The Appellant

Based on a True Story, sort of...

The characters and events depicted in this story are fictitious. Any similarity to actual persons, living or dead is purely coincidental. The people and organizational names have been changed to protect the many in Mila's past, present and future, as well as, the past, present and future of many others involved or not. Any and all public places and locations were used briefly to set the time and framework of the events in the story. The order of events might be nearly accurate, yet the points of views are pretty close.

I, Mila, reserve to me all my rights and permissions of this story and protected for me so that the complete true story one day may be revealed and shared as it should. Only those Behind Closed Doors know the truth. Until then, please read my story, and take the time to slow down from the rat race we live in to consider how it can help you and others. Amen.

MILAGROS RAYRAY

Copyright © 2016, 2017, 2018 MILAGROS RAYRAY

Cover Images © iStock
#689223424, #469979191, #518899548

ISBN: 1545370575

ISBN-13: 978-1545370575

Volume 1 Series 1 Issue 1

The Appellant - The Pilot Episode "Mila's Story"

Twitter Handles: @PardonMila @MilaRayRay

Facebook: http://facebook.com/TheAppellant

Website: http://www.TheAppellant.com/

PURPOSE & DISCLAIMER

The Appellant is of great public interest. It will help the public better understand the due process, or lack thereof in Mila's experience being indicted for elderly abuse and exploitation. This story will explore what happened from her point of view; the process, actions, and possible errors in the medical and judicial system regarding elderly care litigation. This is a growing problem that has yet to be optimized and streamlined for the defense and the prosecution. While there are two sides to any story, each side of Mila's story and many other stories should be revealed.

In this case, my case, her truth was not revealed. While Mila does regret that while she was partially wrong by perception or misunderstood facts, she was mostly right. She wished there could have been a more honest approach, discussion and communication through her entire experience and situation.

English is such a poor language to communicate. For Mila, it was not her first and primary language. In her case, Tagalog was her first language and at the time of her story, her English was not so great, and her frustration and anger in the communication barrier in the lack of legal-ease in processes with all the organizations was predominantly her downfall.

This book is about asking for justice in the truth and how it can help others avoid the challenges and injustice Mila experienced. In the end and for the rest of her life, she will not be bitter, vengeful or sad, just happy to know she can tell the whole and complete truth and let others know that through great trials -- tribulation exists.

DISCLAIMER, TERMS & AGREEMENTS

Anyone who purchases, possesses or receives this book by any means, your acceptance of this book you agree to not do, act or file anything against anyone for things like slander, libel, copyright or trademark or other legal challenges; however one is allowed the opportunity to submit revisions and improvements for the next revision as new and other appellants come forward. The due diligence it took to research this book and write it under free and protected speech was done to the best of one's abilities, counsel, and resources.

FIRST IMPRESSIONS & REVIEWS

"One of the most thought compelling books I have read in the past 25 years regarding elderly litigation. Sad but true. Mila's story is worth a pardon." ~ Tim S. - The Nevada Elderly Law Review

"Mila's story is sadly so true to so many. If you don't have enough money to defend yourself, the prosecution will prevail against you even if you are innocent." ~ Michael A. – The Center against Mass Incarceration

"I firmly believe that Mila has the right to share her story and do so in the most reasonable and prudent manner. Her due diligence to write her story as she experienced it and have it drafted and completed so that anyone can appreciate." Jack S. – Retired Public Defender, Somewhere in the USA

FORWARD BY DREW JACKSON

I have witnessed many injustices in life and while this story was brought to my attention in a short matter of time, it nonetheless deserves a thorough reading and understanding of how the legal and medical system has been fraught with the need for necessary overhaul and improvements in ongoing training, investigative audits on personnel behavior, along with ethics and full transparency.

While this story touches upon these systems in a more direct way from one person's perspective, the overarching situation is that the problem is worsening regarding heavy handed prosecution and heavy handed investigative techniques used to punish the public rather than preventatively curb and protect the elderly and help small medium and large organizations continue to provide positive care.

Mila's story as The Appellant shatters the ice and creates a ground breaking framework for others to tell their story. Enjoy the pages. The research was pretty good. Given more time the story will expand and adapt to those who speak up about their own experiences, successes and failures. I definitely appreciate the bravery it took Mila to stand up and share her story.

MILA'S DEDICATION

This book has been written and dedicated to my children. I want to thank my three beautiful daughters; Louraine, Cheryl and Vanessa, for their love and understanding. With the three of my daughters, I am able to tell my story and write this book. With all my heart, passion, and love was to give each of them the very best. I want to thank God, his only son Jesus, and my Holy Spirit for the enduring energy and guidance to live on through all of these experiences I am about to share with you.

MILA'S ACKNOWLEDGMENTS

I am deeply grateful for my family and friends who have stood by me through all the good and bad times. I am equally thankful for my team of reviewers and editors, and legal helpers who have taken the time out of their busy schedule to provide their wisdom and feedback.

My journey from the Philippines to America where I have been blessed and challenged throughout my life could not be done without the help of so many. I love my Mom and I love my family and continue to give all I can to their health and happiness. This book might help those in need beyond hopes, wishes and life.

Last but not least, there is a person who saw something good in me. His name is Andy. He could sense the truth in me and knew it was worth sharing both carefully, reasonably and prudently. He believed the benefits of sharing my story outweighed the risks. As long as the truth is told and in the way story I believe happened, then no harm will come and only good will be returned and the truth revealed.

All my life I have been dedicated to the selfless care of the elderly. I have always served in good faith. Though I was low, He lifts me up.

For those of you who have had similar situations and going through the very same, this book might help you endure and understand the frustration I experienced and suffered. In the end one will hopefully be restored to fulfill one's lifelong pursuits and be happy filled with joy, receive grace and many blessings.

TABLE OF CONTENTS

Chapter 1 - LoCheVa — 1

Chapter 2 – Mila, Harry and Brian — 8

Chapter 3 - Brian's Back Story - Literally — 17

Chapter 4 - The First 911 Call — 21

Chapter 5 - St. Catholic's Investigates — 28

Chapter 6 - Mila Confronts Harry — 40

Chapter 7 - Brian's Will — 48

Chapter 8 – Paperwork Day — 51

Chapter 9 – Informing Harry — 57

Chapter 10 – Things Settle Down, Sort of — 60

Chapter 11 – Doctor's Good Check up — 64

Chapter 12 – The State Gets Involved — 70

Chapter 13 – The Slip & Fall Accident — 77

Chapter 14 - The State Investigates Harshly — 97

Chapter 15 – Brian transferred against His will — 108

Chapter 16 – Mila Indicted & Charged — 110

Chapter 17 – Brian Dies in State Custody — 119

Chapter 18 – Change in Legal Defense — 122

Chapter 19 – Wronged by the Jury — 129

Chapter 20 – Sentenced and Unexpectedly Jailed — 131

Chapter 21 – The Parr County Jail — 133

Chapter 22 – The Transfer to Smiley — 136

Chapter 23 – The First Years – No Parole — 144

Chapter 24 – Reasoning through It All — 146

Chapter 25 – Behind Closed Doors with God	149
Chapter 26 – The First Appeals, et al.	151
Chapter 27 – The Appellant is Created & Born	153
Chapter 28 – Mila's Appeals, Denial after Denial	158
Chapter 29 – Released from Smiley	160
Chapter 30 – The Continuation of Faith	164
Chapter 31 – Probation Time	165
Chapter 32 – Highest Denial - US Supreme Court	166
Chapter 33 – So as it was lived, it will be written	168
Chapter 34 – Mila meets someone unexpected	170
Chapter 35 – The truth will be revealed	173
Chapter 36 – The re-encounter with the defense	175
Chapter 37 – Brian's Wishes	182
Chapter 38 – Epilogue & Moral of the Story	184
Chapter 39 – Law Students, Judges, Investigators	189
Chapter 40 – Open Questions - Closed Answers	191
Chapter 41 – Timeline of Events – Important Dates	194
Chapter 42 – The Pilot Episode - Screen Play	195
Chapter 42 – The End	196

THE APPELLANT

Chapter 1 - LoCheVa

It was May 2006 and Mila was just getting dressed for the day. She had a flair for wearing the right clothes for the right situation and looking just perfect. Mila was an elderly caregiver and small business owner, always dressed professionally and appropriately for her patients and her caregivers. Mila's real story does not really start here, but for the moment this is where the story begins in this chapter of her life.

Mila had three children. Each was somewhere in their lives doing what they wanted to do and what needed to be done. Loreena, Mila's oldest, was living in California. Cherise, her middle daughter was going to the local university, and her youngest Valerie was in elementary school still living at home.

Mila had three home care facilities closely located to each other in Sparks Nevada that she tended to daily. Mila's company was named after her daughters - LoCheVa. LoCheVa was a group of three homes in beautiful little city named Sparks.

Between work and raising children, Mila's hands were full with responsibility. Each and every day Mila had a routine that she dedicated herself to, getting everyone up and going, fed, and out the door and doing something wonderful.

Valerie her youngest was still living at home and just stirring in bed when Mila came by her bedroom door and yelled,

"Valerie! Time to get up!"

Valerie likes to sleep in. Mila was not in the mood again for Valerie's antics. Of course, Valerie was only 6 years old and what else does a 6 year old do but challenge her mother all day long and night. Today was no exception.

For Valerie, she was young, presumptuous and was not in the mood to hear her mother yelling to get up, and she just rolled over like normal. Being only 6 years old she was a bit of a handful for her mother. Her room was not the cleanest or tidiest of room but it was colorful. It was painted in pretty pink and white colors and fresh pillows and stuffed animals that were just enough to cover half her bed.

"Valerie!" Mila yelled one more time as she walked down the hallway picking up odds and ends in the hallway that somehow got left there the day before. Mila really did not understand how her third child could be so messy when her other two were not even close to being so unorganized. Why the trait of being tidy did not rub off on her youngest? It could be that Valerie was an "oops" in terms of planning. Her oldest Loreena and second oldest Cherise both had impeccable neatness and were nearly 16 years older. Mila did not expect to have a third child. Nevertheless, Valerie was one of the brightest kids in her neighborhood and that made Mila a very proud Mom.

Valerie stirred a bit more and finally rolled out of bed and yelled, "I'm up Mom! It's too early!" She rolled back over and wanted to stay in bed but she knew her Mom would not be happy.

Mila heard Valerie as she finished up things in the hallway and headed to the kitchen.

Mila yelled one more time, "Get dressed!"

THE APPELLANT

Oh well Valerie thought to herself. Little did she know her life was about to get turned upside down because her Mom was going to meet and help a new client that month that was going to change the course of her childhood, as well as, unfortunately the future and present life of her Mom's entire family.

Valerie went ahead and got up and started her day getting ready for school. She was very picky and very-very disorganized. She grabbed some sweats and threw those on, and grabbed her school books and other things and jammed them into her backpack, and yanked her cell phone off the charger, and that was all she needed. She headed to the door to catch up with her Mom.

Mila finished her morning tidying up and was busy getting ready to tend to all her patients at all her residences. She knew her caretakers may have had a busy night doing their work and she was nonetheless ready to make sure all was ready and prepared for the day. But first she had to get Valerie off to school.

"Babyko, get in the car. I'm running late." Mila said.

Valerie butted back at her Mom, "All right Mom, slow down. You're always late."

They both headed out the door and to the garage to get into Mila's 4Runner. They both buckled up and headed down the street to Valerie's school. Not too late, but just about on time as usual.

After Mila dropped Valerie off at school she stopped to look at her cell phone. Just a few messages and those were not too important. Today like any other day, Mila was expecting to go see a patient. Mila looked out the car window while driving back and the spring rain had just fallen on the streets and yards around the homes in the area. It smelled good. The sun was about to come out as well and make everything nice and warm. It was definitely a nice spring morning to run errands.

Mila returned home and was still getting things ready for her day when the phone rang. Her niece Pia called and reminded Mila they had a new patient to visit across the valley and wanted Mila to join her. Mila was definitely up for a new patient and would definitely enjoy the short trip from Sparks across the Truckee River. It would only take 15 minutes to get there. The break from all the early work taking care of patients would be well earned.

Pia was busy doing this and that within her home of patients and definitely wanted to make sure everyone was happy and taken care of. Mila like Pia were the same in their seriousness to be of service and do so with much professionalism. Their daily duty of happily serving and taking care of the elderly was their lifelong passion. Both of them were from the Philippines and it is an honor to care for the old and aging. It is not a duty taken lightly. It is the nature of their culture, a loving and giving, helping culture.

It was early afternoon when Mila picked up Pia agreed to meet and go visit the potential new patient. Hidden Valley was not far away. Pia was relatively new to the US so her English was not so good, yet Mila had lived in the US since 1986 and was in so-so command of the English language except many of the nuances in it. Pia and Mila often spoken in Taglish while in private and among friends; Taglish the combination of English and Tagalog. As they drove along they chit chatted about this and that and what they were going to make for dinner. It was something zesty and tasty, and definitely from Marlokita's International Store.

THE APPELLANT

Marlokita's was their favorite local Filipino store located not far from home just down on Kietzke Avenue. Mila and Pia continued to talk about what they could have for dinner while they were on their way not knowing much about how in a few months their life would be changing for the worse.

As they pulled down the country road into Hidden Valley, the golf course on the right was busy with golfers and those enjoying spring season on the greens. Neither Mila nor Pia were avid golfers yet they enjoyed their patients who had loved the game and watched it on television and spoke of how they loved it when they were younger and able to enjoy the greens.

No sooner than they got into the heart of Hidden Valley, they found the street they were going to find their future patient. They patient's name was Emily and she was in need of part time one-on-one care for two days a week. Within a few minutes they pulled into the driveway of the Emily's address and parked. Getting out of the car they noticed the beautiful flower bed and the neatly kept hedges along with some pretty wind chimes that gently played in the breeze.

Mila and Pia knocked on the door and after a brief moment a young woman answered the door and said hello, and introduced herself as Emily's daughter.

She was polite and let them in and asked if they had any problems finding the address. Mila and Pia said they enjoyed short drive and no problems finding her and asked how Emily was feeling.

Emily's daughter walked them into the living room where Emily was seated and Mila and Pia sat down. It was a lovely room and the sunshine was shining in on the coffee table where some small pretty figurines were placed.

Mila and Pia asked Emily how she was feeling and she said could be doing better and asked about their background and if they were available to the part time care she needed. Of course, Mila and Pia replied and asked a few questions about which days of the week and what specific items out of the ordinary would Emily need.

Emily said it was not much, just help during the days when her daughter was in school and at work on the same day and not able to give her assistance with getting around the house.

The house was pretty large and spacious with hardwood furniture and white carpet and everything was neatly kept. Emily had no pets to take care of hair and dust was not really present. Emily could not drive so most of the errands for home items and food were taken care of by her daughter. Emily asked if Mila and Pia were able to cook and obtain groceries for those few days and of course they replied yes. That was good. Emily said she needed help mostly in the morning, and she did not need a walker or a cane, yet just a little help was always appreciated. By the afternoon her aching bones were warmed up enough to not need help yet she loved to still have company to enjoy the rest of each day.

So Mila and Pia was happy to discuss their services and benefits for which Emily appreciated and her daughter only asked a few questions. Everything seemed good, so Mila and Pia decided to thank them and gave Emily their contact information and said they would give her a call tomorrow to see if they had any questions and when they could begin to offer their help. Emily did not need to wait and said she was grateful for them to start and said the beginning of

THE APPELLANT

next week would be perfect. They politely shook hands and Emily's daughter walked them to the front door and thanked them again for taking the time to come visit. Mila and Pia walked outside and again thanked Emily's daughter and walked to their car in the driveway.

It was only a few moments while they paused to get in the car and a man on a walk going by said hello to them and asked them how their day was, and they answered it was beautiful. Mila mentioned they were visiting a potential new patient and he replied in interest if they offered residential home care, and they both replied yes. Harry, his name, introduced himself and said he had a friend who was in need, and he was the current guardian of a man named Brian. In a week or so, Brian was to be discharged and he needed an elderly group home to stay in.

Mila and Pia mentioned they could set up a time to visit and learn more. Harry liked the idea and they exchanged numbers in the driveway and of Mila and Pia then got in their car and went back to Sparks to follow-up with their current patients and tend to the rest of the day.

MILAGROS RAYRAY

Chapter 2 – Mila, Harry and Brian

A day later, Harry called Mila and said he would like to visit her residence and see if Brian would like it. Mila said she would be pleased to show him, and they arranged for that morning for him to visit and check things out. Harry was rather excited to find something so quickly.

A few hours later Harry arrived and walked up and Mila showed him around the LoCheVa residence. Mila had always kept things nice and clean, tidy and organized for any unexpected guests. Harry was quite pleased with everything he saw and mentioned Brian would love to relocate as soon as possible. Mila and Harry discussed possible terms of providing care and shook hands and agreed to then meet Brian. Off Harry went and Mila was also happy to be of great service.

Two days later Harry called and asked to have Mila and Pia come visit Brian at the care facility. It was called Monument Care Skilled Nursing Facility. Harry said his friend's name was Brian and he could arrange an evaluation and assessment. Mila needed to determine and confirm how much assistance Brian might need. He could require a little or a lot of care and that would determine monthly costs. All seemed well and good to Mila.

It was Friday morning and the sun was coming up as Mila arrived at Monument Care. She walked in, and checked in, and Harry had already arrived earlier to meet up with Brian for breakfast. Tomorrow was the day he was to check out and Harry had one day to find something suitable for Brian and he hoped Mila would be the perfect fit.

THE APPELLANT

Brian in his room was up and his bones were aching a bit, and his medication was near his bed stand. Harry gave him something for his pain and put the medication away so as to not knock it over during breakfast.

Brian was feeling well aside from his back pains as Mila was being escorted to his room. Harry looked up to meet her and said good morning. Brian, a slightly tall 82 year old Italian had a warm smile and said good morning to Mila. Mila greeted him and asked him how he felt this morning. He was good. Harry said they were just getting to breakfast and that the timing was perfect. Brian and Harry described that basic home care like assistance with bathing, board and lodging and some help getting up and around, nothing out of the ordinary. So Mila, Harry and Brian agreed the rate would be the normal. Mila said the rate would only change if more care would be required and Brian said that would not be necessary. They both smiled and said great. They could move the next day on Sunday around noon.

Everything felt great to all. Overall, Brian was feeling well enough, coherent and alert to answer questions about what he needed most and what he did not require. Mila was most polite and happy to offer him a nice solution.

Sunday came and around noon, Brian was discharged and released. The Monument Care staff was happy to see Brian go and get a more comfortable living arrangement. Harry had packed Brian's small amount of belongings, mostly clothes and mementos, along with his medications. They both wrapped up things and then headed out to Harry's car, got in and headed out following Mila to her care home.

Brian was very happy to find a place that would be so much nicer than a sterile care facility. In a home that was warm and cozy he knew he would be happier. Instead of food that was tasteless and staff that was non-human like, he wanted to be back in a real home where he knew he would be treated with more dignity and with more respect.

It was sunny Sunday afternoon and Brian with Harry's help drove up to Mila's care home and parked in the driveway. It was called LoCheVa Residential Care Home. Brian liked the fact that the name of the home was based on each of Mila's daughters; Loreena, Cherise, Valerie. It was a pretty name and Mila was very proud of it as she told Brian and Harry as she walked in ahead of them.

For Harry and Brian settling in was easy. They walked up the front of the residence and noticed how pretty the yard was, the windows were clean and flowers were blooming. The door handle was a beautiful brass shiny color. As they walked in, they noticed two residents were in the living room enjoying a cup of coffee and some tea while watching television. One of them was Joseph a resident and patient, and Jane who was a close friend renting one of the rooms as a boarder, and they both were aware Brian was moving in and were happy to meet someone new. They both smiled and said hello to Brian.

Mila had prepared him a nice room with all the things that fit him for his needs. A cozy and semi-firm bed just to his liking, a chair, a night stand and lamp, a television on a stand, a rectangular wide alpine lattice window with a view of the backyard, as well as, his own private bathroom to the left in his room. There were a few pictures and mirrors hanging on a beautifully satin colored wall and a ceiling fan to give the room a cool quiet and warm soothing feeling.

THE APPELLANT

There was no hum from the fan as it slowly turned, and a nice spring warm feeling from the sunshine coming through the window.

Harry finished helping Brian unpack and arrange his things; and his clothes and mementos around the room. He was quite pleased with how spacious the room was and how neat and bright it was. The curtains were thick and heavy to help keep the light out if it got too bright. His medications Mila took and reviewed and stored in a dry cool place for him in the private cabinet in the kitchen. These were his daily medications other than the things he needed in his room during the week.

Mila checked in on the other patients while Harry checked out the place for himself. Brian thought Harry was right that this was a perfect place for him to be taken care of.

While Brian scooted around the residence, his back start to ache again, and he looked for his medication and took his prescribed dosage. Mila had placed his medication where he could find it in the kitchen at just the right spot. Little did Mila know that Brian over the past few months had an increase in back pain that he was hiding and not mentioning, even to Harry his guardian. All the while, Brian continued to keep to himself about it, and figured his pain would subside eventually.

The afternoon came quickly and Harry and Mila had finished their discussions on next steps for Brian. Harry said he would come back tomorrow morning and check on Brian and bring a few other things that Brian had in storage that would make his visit happier.

Brian decided to settle down for the evening in the living room along with Joseph and Jane who were happy watching a movie.

Mila earlier had started to simmer something in the kitchen that was starting to fill the house with a beautiful aroma. Harry said he needed to get going so he left Brian in the living room and headed off. Mila gave a nice smile to Harry as he walked out the front door, and she went on to check on everyone to see what they needed. All were happy and content. Mila decided to make some tea for everyone to enjoy and went into the kitchen. The evening was beginning nicely. That was all about to change.

At about 9pm, Jane, Joseph and Brian were in their rooms getting ready to go to sleep when Brian came out and asked for his medication. Mila had already given him what he was allowed for the day and she asked if he was in any discomfort. Brian just noted his back was bothering him again and that he needed something to help him sleep. Mila offered something other than his prescribed medication and he was happy with that. Mila returned to her late night duties and Brian returned to his room to head off to sleep.

With Joseph, Jane and Brian all destined to sleep and rest, Mila went into her study to finish writing up patient notes and logbook entries to wrap up the day. It was a good day. All seemed perfect with everyone tucked in and settled in. Mila decided to take a small nap in the living room and listen for any patient needs before going to her bedroom for the night. An hour passed and Mila decided to go to sleep and wrapped up her things and turned down the lights, leaving the hallway light and kitchen lights on, checking to see everything was locked and the drapes were closed.

About 1am, Mila was awoken by Brian as he walked to her bedroom door, and he said he needed his back pain medication. Mila was surprised that Brian needed another dosage when he was given a dosage right before he got into bed around 9pm, and prior to that his

THE APPELLANT

5pm dinner dosage. Mila thought his request seemed odd and looked at the time and noticed it was too early in the morning for such a request. So, she got up and helped Brian to the reclining chair in the living room. Brian winced a little and said his back was killing him. She was concerned so she went and looked at his medication and it indicated and allowed a dose once per 4 hours as needed. She got him his dosage with a glass of water and he downed the pills quickly.

Brian said that would do and got up and she helped him back to his bedroom and arranged his bedding and helped him get back into bed. He winced again and she made sure he was made comfortable. He seemed okay and she wished him a good night and to get some rest. He nodded and she let herself out of his room leaving the door cracked open. She went back to her desk and made a note in her logbook, and then back to her bedroom and returned to sleep.

About 30 minutes later, Brian yelled from his room asking for help insisting that he needed another pain pill. Mila quickly rushed to his room and said the dosage she gave him was all she could give per the doctor's orders. That would not do for Brian and she did not know it. She reluctantly instructed him to try and arrange himself to get as comfortable as possible. Brian did not sleep for the rest of the night.

In the morning, Mila was still in the living room on the couch and she had listened to Brian all night, and Joseph and Jane had come out and heard him all night and asked Mila what they were going to do. She told them she had a call into Brian's doctor office regarding what was happening and for a recommendation. Mila had talked to the nurse, and the nurse reached out to the doctor and he agreed to double the dosage and reached out to the pharmacy to authorize the prescription. Later Monday morning, Mila called Harry and he went to the pharmacy to get the prescription and then went to the residence to drop it off and handed it to Mila and she verified the prescription. Mila was hoping the raised dosage would help him to get to sleep.

For the rest of the day Brian seemed okay, and Joseph and Jane enjoyed their afternoon bite to eat with Brian in the kitchen. Pia had come over around 2PM and was helping Mila with an early dinner and some cleaning items when Mila mentioned the previous night's experience. Pia was surprised and wondered if she could help. Mila shared that the doctor had increased Brian's prescription dosage and that should help.

The second night came quickly around 8pm and it was worse that the first night. Joseph and Jane each had enjoyed dinner and was settling in, and Brian had eaten a little but showed signs of uncomfortable pain as he moved around. Mila and Pia were not sure what to do except to help him get ready for bed.

All was settled until suddenly they heard Harry yelling for them because he was in terrible pain. Brian was worse than expected to both of them. Brian was given his dosage of medication and still he was screaming in pain. All night they tended to him and tried to comfort him with warm and cooling pads and trying to position him so he would not wince, and they realize they were not going to get any sleep that night. They knew they must do something and to help and remedy Brian's dilemma.

The morning came quickly, and both Mila and Pia were exhausted. They got both Jane and Joseph something ready for breakfast in the kitchen and they took Brian something because he

THE APPELLANT

was not able to move. They barely survived the night, and the next morning they called Harry the first chance they got.

Mila explained to Harry that they could not care for Brian because his chronic back pain was not explained to them when they accepted him into their residence. His needs far exceeded their ability to help him. They needed to get him to a facility where he could be treated for his incredible back pain under the observation and care of a doctor and medical team.

They were worried Brian could really hurt himself under their care. Mila and Pia were very tired and needed to make sure they got Brian the help he needed very soon. They checked with Harry later that Tuesday morning and he came over and checked with Brian. Brian said he did not want to go back to any care facility and wanted to stay where he was. Harry could not convince Brian to return to any other facility.

Mila and Pia were beside themselves and only could surmise that Brian was going to need extra attention. Three more days and nights had passed with the same experience as the first. Now it had been four days and things were only getting worse. Pia and Mila were not getting any sleep at night and Brian was constantly in pain.

The situation was impossible. Mila decided to contact Harry and Brian and indicate they needed to raise the monthly rate if this continues. Both Harry and Brian knew something would have to change. Brian did not have enough from his retirement to cover much more than what he was paying, and Harry started to realize that maybe being at LoCheVa was not going to be a good idea even after one day of Brian's complaints. But then again, Brian liked being there instead of a nursing home. Frustration was building in everyone.

Thursday came and everyone during the day continued as usual and Jane and Joseph were happy to enjoy the afternoon quietly in the living room eating some snacks and light appetizers that Mila and Pia had prepared prior to dinner. Brian was in his room resting and munching on some of the appetizers that Mila had brought to him. He really liked the special care he was getting.

Dinner finally came around 6pm, and Brian came out of his room and joined everyone in the kitchen while Mila set out the dishes and silverware. Pia finished the entrees and placed them out. Joseph and Jane relished a nice hot dinner and the fresh vegetables were their favorite. Brian after a few days really enjoyed the three hot meals during the day, and this was no exception. His back was still aching but not as much as the day before. Everyone chatted about this and that at dinner and ended on a good note and retired to the living room. Brian was especially happy and told Mila and Pia how much he loved being there instead of the nursing home.

Around 9pm, Brian and everyone decided to call it a night and Mila and Pia got everyone their evening prescription medication as directed and tucked everyone into bed. Mila and Pia thought the night was going to be relaxing. That was the opposite of what was about to happen.

Mila and Pia decided to go to sleep and wrapped up their notes and log entries in their office and turned off the extra lights and cleaned up the kitchen and headed to bed right around 10PM.

It was about 12:30am and Brian turned in his bed and his medication was wearing off faster than he thought. He winced and

THE APPELLANT

of course he had been hiding the real pain for nearly three days but the threshold of tonight's pain unlike other nights escalated more quickly. What was Brian going to do?

MILAGROS RAYRAY

Chapter 3 - Brian's Back Story - Literally

Little did anyone know that over the past few months, Brian's pain was nearly intolerable and his guardian Harry had a good idea but never let on that he knew or realized Brian's pending threshold would be too much stand for Mila and Pia to manage. The medication was being consumed faster than normal and with the dosage being doubled; Harry knew someone might notice sooner than later.

Mila and Pia did not have long to wait because by 1 AM Brian was in terrible pain and his threshold was beyond his wits. He decided not to wake Mila or Pia and made his way to the kitchen and found his prescription bottle and started to take a few more pills with a glass of water. He made his way back to his room and crawled back into bed. His pain was not subsiding yet. It was 1:30AM and the clock just ticked ever so slowly. He looked at the ceiling with his nightlight and it was just strong enough for him to make out the room in the dark.

Brian's eyes were wide open and he remembered back over the last few months when the pain was terrible and his nursing care staff would not tolerate him anymore. How did he come to this place where he did not want the pain anymore and he was unhappy to bother so many caring people with his medical needs? His clock in his room that he brought from his home was on the wall and it ticked ever so slowly. The clock hands almost seemed to stop as his pain continued to increase. All he could focus on was his pain.

He knew if he complained to Mila or Pia anymore he would surely have to be moved, and all of what he had come to was an end. None of them knew his pain. Even Harry was not aware. The night

THE APPELLANT

before he felt good that he had comfort and attention but he knew that his agonizing was not going to get rid of the brutal pain in his back. He wanted to end his life and though Harry was slightly aware of his suicidal comments in the past few months, he was not sure how much Harry was going to understand if he took his own life.

The clock hands ticked again like hammers hitting a railroad tie. In his mind, his body needed relief. It was nearly 2AM and it was quiet in the house. He decided this was it; he wanted to end it, end it all. He painfully rolled over in his bed, and managed to get his feet to the floor without slipping. He grabbed the night stand with one hand and steadied himself. He reached over and grabbed his robe and slipped it on. Oh the pain. One foot after the other he made his way to his bedroom door, and then a few more steps to the hallway. He stopped, and listened. He could hear no noise from Jane or Joseph who were quietly sleeping and briefly snoring.

Mila's room was further down off to the left of the kitchen, so he probably would not be noticed. He made his way to the kitchen, and did not turn on the light. He used the nightlight that was on the wall to see his way and edge his way near his medicine cabinet where his prescribed pain killers were stored. The cabinet creaked as he started to open it so he paused to make sure no one heard his movements. Brian did not hear anyone notice his movements so he continued to open the cabinet and looked for his pain meds, and took the whole bottle and put it in his pocket and then closed the cabinet slowly.

He made his way slowly back to his room. Once inside, he knew what he was going to do. The clock ticked again hard enough for him to look over and see that it was 2:25AM. He was going to take enough pills to end the pain. He was not absolutely sure how much it would take, but the double dosage was not working. Brian knew that two to three times the dosage might work to kill him. His pain was just too unbearable to drag anyone else along with him anymore. Going back to a nursing home or medical care facility was not an option. Dying pain free away from the hospital or acute care center is the only option. Harry would not be pleased, but then again Harry argued with him about ending his life over the past few months and neither of them saw eye to eye on his level of pain and suffering. Brian knew it was a matter of time before anyone realized how bad he really was feeling.

Depressed and in anguish, Brian took a handful of pain pills and the glass of water next to his night stand and swallowed all of them and chugged two gulps of water. That was it. No more pain would he feel again and though he was looking around the room to remember where he was and how he felt, he knew it would not take long. The clock ticked again and this time he realized how much the only thing he would not miss was the ticking of any clock.

Bong, the clock chimed 2:30AM and he had never noticed or heard the half hour sound before. It must have meant something special for his moments and time were at hand. He thought about Joseph and Jane in the other room and Mila down the hall, everyone resting and he could only think that his pain was slowly fading. He pulled his blanket up and laid down on his back resting his head on his pillow and looked up and closed his eyes. He took a deep breath and relaxed. It felt good to relax and his back pain was drifting away.

The morning came and it was 7 AM. Mila got up and put on her robe and walked into the kitchen and filled the tea pot with water and placed it on the stove. Mila found her cell phone and noticed a few text messages and no missed calls. She went to find her glasses

THE APPELLANT

so she could read them. Nothing important she noted as she read her messages.

Mila then went down the hallway and Joseph and Jane's doors were closed and Brian's door was cracked open. She looked inside and she could see Brian in bed asleep. She continued down the hallway to the hallway bathroom and her glasses were not there either. So she came back and peeked into Brian's room and noticed his blanket was not covering him very well so she approached the bed to straighten his covers and turned over a throw blanket and found his bottle of pain killers. The lid was not on it and she picked it up and it felt very light, too light.

Her eyes batted quickly at him lying there and said his name. "Brian, Brian! Brian!!" No answer. This was not right. She said again, "Brian, Brian". Again no answer, she immediately went to his side and put her hand on his shoulder and he did not move. She was in terror now and rolled him over and he was barely breathing. His skin was cold and his mouth was open wide and she could see his lips were dry. She knew immediately what had happened and went straight for the telephone in the hallway.

What was about to happen next was the beginning for which there should have been a different ending.

MILAGROS RAYRAY

Chapter 4 - The First 911 Call

It was 7:30 AM -- Mila dialed 911 and an emergency operator answered within a second, "911- What is your emergency?"

"This is Mila RayRay at 60 Suzanne Way in Sparks, and one of my patients has overdosed!" Mila shouted. "Can you please send help?" She ran back to the bedroom and shook Brian several times. He was barely breathing and his skin was cold. The 911 operator still had Mila on the phone and she responded, "Yes, ma'am can you confirm your telephone number and who is overdosed?" Mila replied, "My number is 775-525-2830, and his name is Brian and he is one of my patients I care for."

Brian was not dead but definitely overdosed. The clock in Brian's room on the wall ticked 7:25 AM. For Mila the time stood still. The 911 Operator's eye batted as she looked at the screen while she was typing feverishly requesting an emergency ambulance in the vicinity to go into response mode.

The 911 operator asked, "Can you confirm the address?" and Mila replied, "60 Suzanne Way Sparks". The operator finished the emergency request and response team emergency action message on her screen confirmed the alert was sent and received.

On the corner of Prater Way and McCarran Boulevard an ambulance had just finished a call thirty minutes prior and was re-organizing for the next alert when their computer monitor flashed a red banner alert with Mila's 911 call details. Tim the rookie driver was only two years on the crew, and Cheryl a seasoned 10 year medical veteran was seated in the passenger seat, and they both looked at the message and went into action. Emergency lights on,

THE APPELLANT

seat belts confirmed on, their white and red emergency life recovery unit (ELCU) rolled out of the parking lot, turned west on Prater Way crossing west McCarran and slipped through the intersection quickly. Cheryl reached over and pressed a button confirming their status. The onboard GPS and alert system already notified the dispatch and control center Tim and Cheryl's response confirmation.

The 911 operator asked Mila, "Do you know what he took?" and Mila replied, "He took most of his pain medication and he is cold and barely breathing." The 911 operator asked what kind and Mila could not read the label since she did not have her glasses on, but she knew what it was by the prescription he was authorized to take. His name was clearly on the label of the bottle.

7:35 AM in the morning and Mila could hear a siren in the distance down the street. She knew it would not be long, and she checked both of Brian's eyes, and his pupils were dilated and responsive and his finger nails when she pinched and released them showed blood returning to his nails. He was not too far gone, but bad enough.

The ambulance arrived within a few more minutes and pulled up and Tim and Cheryl jumped into action. Each of them grabbed an EMT tackle kit and jogged up the walkway to the door. Mila was standing in the doorway and let them.

"He is in the first room down the hallway on the right." Mila said. Tim and Cheryl both hurried down and into the bedroom and set their equipment down and immediately got on both sides of Brian. They checked his pulse and his pupils just as Mila had done thirty minutes prior. They were able to verify Brian was overdosed. They quickly placed an oxygen mask on him to stabilize his breathing and rechecked his pupils and pulse. His eyes were responsive and his blood pressure was shallow yet he was alive. They knew he would make it but they needed to get him to the hospital quickly.

Outside the fire department had just arrived, sirens blaring as they came down the street, just minutes behind the ambulance. The firemen were well versed in how to help the ambulance team and had retrieved a gurney from the ambulance and were already bringing it into the house and down the hall. The two residents Joseph and Jane were in the hallway with Pia watching them hurry in. Mila was still with Cheryl and Tim in Brian's room. The two firemen secured the gurney next to Brian's bed and everyone quickly pulled the sheets out from the bed and picked up Brian and placed him on the gurney carefully.

Cheryl said to Mila, "Follow us to the hospital. We are going to St. Catholic's Hospital. Grab Brian's prescribed medication and bring it." Mila understood and quickly left the room and into the kitchen and grabbed Brian's other medications from the cabinet. She ran to her bedroom and quickly changed into some sweats and shoes while the firemen and Cheryl and Tim moved Brian out to the ambulance. Pia and the residents were coming down the hallway too wondering if there was anything they could do.

Mila ran out the door, "Just stay here and I'll call you." Pia nodded and replied, "Ok Mila. Go! Go! Let me know." Mila's ran to her car as the ambulance pulled away and the firemen put away their gear and started to load up. Mila in her car was not far behind when the ambulance rushed down Prater way to get on the freeway to get to St. Catholic's Hospital. St. Catholic's was just three miles away. It was one of three medical hospitals in the area. It was the best hospital in the area in comparison to the county hospital or the primary acute care hospital, and it was close and good enough for immediate care.

Tim and Cheryl pulled the ambulance up to the St. Catholic's emergency ramp and they quickly parked and unloaded Brian as a small ER team rushed to help. The ER team was alerted and was standing by with overdose treatment medication. The ER doors opened and Brian was still unconscious. Mila was right behind and pulled in the ER entrance and parked out of the way and near the ER doors and rushed in with Brian's medication. The ER lobby was bright with fluorescent lights and sterile white in color.

The front desk nurse saw Mila rushing in and asked, "Who are you?" and Mila pointed at Brian on the gurney and replied "I am his care giver, and here are all his meds." The nurse quickly took the bottles and looked at the medication and on a clipboard started noting the label information.

The nurse asked, "What's his name and age?" Mila replied, "Brian , age 82" Mila was watching over the counter at the ER team working on Brian not far away, and knew that she could not go into the ER room.

"Is he allergic to anything?"

"No, nothing" Mila replied. Mila reached for her telephone and dialed Pia's number.

The nurse looked over her shoulder and she could see the ER team had slowed down on their work and realized Brian was stabilized and their teams were past the dangerous and scary part.

"Pia" Mila said. "I am here at the hospital and they are working on Brian." Pia said to Mila that Joseph and Jane were concerned about Brian. Mila could tell from the nurse's expression that Brian was going to be okay and relayed that to Pia. She realized that Harry his guardian needed to be contacted immediately as well and she made the call to him.

It was 6:30am and the sun was coming up and Harry was in his kitchen just getting his wallet and keys after sipping some coffee before he headed to work. Harry's home was in Hidden Valley next door to Brian's existing home. As Harry was just headed out the door, the telephone rang.

Harry picked up the phone and answered, "Hello."

Mila replied, "Harry, its Mila. Brian tried to kill himself this morning and we are at the hospital."

"What! When? Where is he now?" Harry frantically replied.

"At St. Catholic's" Mila explained.

Harry quickly pulled the power cord on the coffee maker and replied, "I am on my way and I will be there in 10 minutes or less." He slammed the phone down and ran out the door.

Mila hung up and looked around. She could see the ER teams slowly breaking down from the ordeal after Brian was stabilized. One of the ER team members was a doctor. She could not make out his name, but he soon gave everyone thumbs up and walked towards the nurse's station.

"Mila?" said the doctor as he approached. "My name is Doctor James Halston. Brian is now stable and out of trouble."

THE APPELLANT

"Oh thank goodness" Mila replied.

"We are going to move Brian out of ER to a hospital room for observation. Do you know why Brian tried to kill himself?"

"I have no idea" Mila replied. "He has only been in my care for a few days."

"I see. He overdosed on his pain medications and it looks intentional. Let me talk with him after he gets settled in his room."

"Ok." Mila stayed in the ER nursing station for a little while longer. She texted Pia to let her know what was going on. She realized Harry would be arriving soon. As she finished her text to Pia she told the ER nurse she was going to move her car from the ER emergency entrance parking and if a man named Harry showed up she would be right back.

Harry was only a few minutes away as Mila came back from the parking lot to the ER nurses station. She could see Harry pulling in and parking near her car and walked up inside ER.

"Hi Harry."

"Hi Mila, where is Brian? Is he going to be alright?"

"Yes, they are moving him to a room just a little while ago"

"Oh good, do you know what room?"

"No yet."

Mila walked over to the ER nursing station.

"Do you know which room Brian is being moved to?"

The nurse replied, "Yes, he is already moved to room 2105. You can take this hallway to the elevator" pointing to right of where Harry and Mila were standing.

"Thank you." Mila replied.

They both went straight down the hallway and to the elevator and pressed the elevator up button. It only took a few moments for the elevator to open while both of them stood quietly anxious to get to Brian to see him.

The elevator door opened and they both went in and pressed the number two for the second floor.

"Has this happened before?" Mila asked Harry.

"No. Well not really, but Brian said a few weeks back that he could not handle the pain anymore."

"What do you mean?" Mila looked up and eyed Harry.

Brian did not want to stay in a nursing home because they treated him so badly, and he could not get the care he needed because of his chronic back pain.

Moments passed as Mila thought about what just happened. What Harry just said and what she was not told during her assessment of Brian. She sensed trouble.

THE APPELLANT

Chapter 5 - St. Catholic's Investigates

Mila had taken Brian into Locheva Care Home not realizing the actual amount of pain and support Brian was going to need. She had been deceived she felt. Mila was getting really nervous at this point.

Mila quickly looked at Harry and explained "There is no way I can take care of Brian if he is in this much pain. I had no idea and for several nights he has kept everyone up complaining and screaming for more medication."

Harry did not look surprised. He knew what Mila was saying and he knew that Brian needed more help than what he had explained and shared up front to Mila and Pia a few weeks back.

The elevator door opened and Mila looked hard at Harry as she walked out and to the nurse's station where a young man was sitting looking at a computer screen typing away. He was an intern nurse stationed there while the morning staff was coming on for the day. He looked up and stopped what he was doing as Mila and Harry approached.

"Yes, can I help you?"

"Brian Room 2105" Mila replied.

"Oh yes, he just got settled and the doctor is with him. What are your names and are you family?"

"I am Mila and this is Harry Braun. I am his caregiver and this is Brian's legal guardian."

"Very good - Thank you - If you give me just a second." The nurse made a few notes and looked at the time on the clock.

"You both can go see him right now. Just down the hall to your left, fourth door Room 2105."

"Thank you." They both turned and walked to the fourth door and looked in Brian was sitting up in his bed and a doctor had a chart and pen and was taking notes. Brian looked up and over and his eyes made the doctor look over his shoulder.

"Ah yes, come in Mila. I was just talking with Brian." Dr. Halston replied. Mila and Harry both walked in. Harry reached out and introduced himself to the doctor.

"My name is Harry, Brian's guardian"

"Nice to meet you Harry, glad you came. Mila and I just met downstairs in ER."

"Hi Brian" Mila said and walked over to his bedside and held his hand and smiled. Brian's eyes lit up and smiled back.

"What do you think you were doing? You scared us."

Brian replied, "I know. I just can't handle the pain anymore. I did not want to hurt anyone."

Harry stepped in and said, "Brian, why?"

Brian looked into Harry's eyes and said, "You know Harry, the pain. I just need to end it. I can't handle it anymore."

The doctor at this point got the idea of what had happened and needed a few moments with everyone. Harry knew it was only a

THE APPELLANT

matter of time before the truth comes out about Brian's degraded status and his desire not to live. Mila was just getting the idea of what happened and the doctor looked at Mila with eyes strained and tried to focus on what was he was going to do. The doctors looked at each of them and realized more questions were needed.

"Ok. Let's do this. Harry and Mila, I need to speak to both of you in a minute in the hallway. Brian, I need you to take your time and relax. How are you feeling, do you need anything?"

"I am feeling okay, just thirsty."

The doctor reached over to the side of the hospital bed and pressed the nurse station button for assistance.

"Very well, we'll get you something in a minute but for the moment just relax and rest." The doctor then nodded at both Harry and Mila to leave the room. The intern from the nurse station entered the doorway and asked, "Yes, did someone need something?"

The doctor replied, "Yes, please get some room temperature water for Brian and make a note on his chart. He can only have so much water at the moment while his fluids are stabilizing."

"Yes doctor"

Mila, Harry and Doctor Halston stepped out of the room and into the hallway. Brian looked at them and said, "I'll be okay. Thanks doc."

In the hallway the doctor motioned them to a small conference room and walked in.

"Harry, my name is Doctor James Halston. Brian just recovered from a severe overdose of pain medication. It appears he was prescribed this. Has this happened before?"

"No not to my knowledge. Brian has just been in a lot more pain lately and I could not take care of him."

"I see. When did Mila get involved?"

"He was in a nursing home and he did not like that and so I found Mila's business, LoCheVa, and he has been there for the last four days."

Dr. Halston nodded and looked at Mila.

"Dr. Halston, I would like to help Brian, but this is not what I had in mind. He definitely needs to get into some other care." Mila said with great concern.

"Harry, what do you want?" Dr. Halston asked.

"I want Brian to get the care he needs. It's up to Brian."

"Ok. Let me go talk to Brian."

Dr. Halston left them both there in the small conference room as the doctor went back to room 2105 to see Brian. Harry and Mila looked at each other and they both sighed.

"Harry, I cannot help Brian for what he needs for the monthly we agreed to."

"I understand, but you do realize that Brian does not like a nursing home and he can't stay in the hospital."

THE APPELLANT

Harry looked at Mila and realized that what he had tried to not mention about the extra issues that Brian had and needed help with were not going to go away. Brian's overdose was just the beginning and he knew based on previous 911 and ER visits that he had not revealed and told Mila the whole truth.

"Well, Harry. I cannot have Brian in my residence if he is having chronic back pain and needs extra care like this for what we are charging. I definitely can't have Brian return the way things are. He needs more medical attention than what you explained."

Harry was not amused and did not know what to say. "Fine, let's talk with Brian then and see."

In the meantime, Dr. Halston had returned to Brian's room where the intern had fetched some water and was just leaving. The doctor knew that something was missing and he needed to ask Brian a few more questions.

"Hello doc" Brian said.

"Hello Brian. I just left Mila and Harry and we need to figure out what we are going to do with you. Your overdose is a very serious issue."

"I know doc. I am in so much pain and I just want to end it all."

"You know Brian, you cannot do that."

"But doc, you don't understand. The pain medication is not working. I don't want to go back to a nursing home because the care is terrible."

The doctor looked at Brian and chagrined. He knew Harry and Mila were talking at this very moment about what to do. Little did anyone realize that Harry and Mila needed to discuss between all four of them that was not apparent a few weeks back; Brian definitely needed more care than what he purported and the overdose incident was not the whole truth.

"Brian, where do you want to go? You cannot stay here and you do not want to go back to the nursing home."

"I want to go back with Mila to LoCheVa. She is very nice and has been so nice to take care of me. It's nice there."

"You have only been there a few days, how do you know?"

"I just know Doc. I can tell. Mila treats me so nice and the food and care is wonderful."

"Okay. Let's get Mila and Harry back in here and go over things."

Brian nodded and Doctor Halston left the room and rejoined Mila and Harry just as they were finishing up what they needed to decide and discuss.

"Mila and Harry, Brian and I just spoke. Let's join him and talk about what needs to happen."

All three of them walked out of the conference room and across the hall to Brian. Brian smiled as Mila walked in, and gave Harry a little frown. Harry knew Brian was not happy if the truth of the matter was found out.

THE APPELLANT

The doctor started, "Brian said he wants to continue to stay with Mila at LoCheVa. Harry do you have any issues with that?"

"No. I just want Brian to be taken good care of."

Mila looked at Harry and Dr. Halston and spoke up, "I don't want Brian to go back with me to my business. He needs more medical care than what was agreed to."

Doctor Halston looked at Brian and Harry and said, "From my understanding, Brian needs more care and he does not want to go to back to a nursing home. If he wants to stay with Mila at LoCheVa you two have to agree to something."

Harry replied, "We will discuss things with Mila. When can Brian be released?"

"Tomorrow, Saturday, Brian can be released. We are going to keep him under observation and make sure he is stable and then he can return to Mila's care."

"Yes." Brian replied. "I'll be fine."

Doctor Halston looked at Mila and Brian and said, "Tomorrow Brian you will be released. Mila, do you need anything."

Mila was not sure everything was settled. She did not want Brian to return to Locheva given what had just happened. Looking at Brian and the doctor, she was very unsure of taking Brian back and continuing with his care.

"I know Harry means well, but I don't think it would be wise for me to take Brian back. He needs to find a nursing home." Mila knew it was not a good idea to keep Brian and could only mean trouble. Mila had a kind heart and knew Brian liked being at her residence with the other two residents and not some stuffy and sterile nursing home.

Brian looked at Mila and the doctor.

"Doc - I want to go back with Mila and LoCheVa. That's what I want."

The doctor looked at Mila and asked her, "I am perfectly fine with Brian being released back to you. Just let Brian stay the rest of the day and tonight for observation. Is there anything stopping Brian?"

Mila replied to both, "I do not want to take Brian back if this is going to happen again. His chronic back pain needs to be taken care of at a more intensive care facility where his medication can be stronger and he can be monitored hourly."

The doctor looked at the medication that Brian was prescribed on his chart and realized it was strong enough and well suited for Brian yet he knew Mila was right. Harry knew that Mila had already indicated that raising Brian's care rate was necessary if he was going to stay at LoCheVa. The doctor had no other issues other than Brian and Mila agreeing with each other. Harry knew that Brian did not have enough monthly income to cover the rate increase at LoCheVa.

Harry spoke up and said, "I want Brian to go to back to a nursing home."

THE APPELLANT

Mila added, "I agree. The care rate we agreed to and this is going to take considerable more time and attention and you know I need to raise the rate."

The doctor looked at both and then at Brian. Brian rolled his eyes and fired back and said, "Harry, you know I hated the hospital and nursing home and yet you want to go back there."

"It's not your decision. Harry, I sometimes wonder if you care about me or my money. Mila, whatever is needed, we can do. I can sell my home if need be."

Harry did not like what Brian just said and that idea as his guardian and knew now was not the right time to fight Brian on that. He needed to get going to work and knew as guardian he could bring this back up after Brian was released.

"Doc, I need to get going to work. Brian, we need to talk later?" Harry was not happy with how Brian was making his decisions yet the doctor knew to keep his distance.

"Yes, Harry, I'll be fine." Brian was looking perturbed at Harry and not liking how he felt.

Brian blurted, "I don't need Harry's permission. He is my guardian and not in charge of my finances."

Mila did not look as startled as the doctor, but knew that if the doctor objected with Brian returning to LoCheVa then she would know that Brian would be better off at a nursing home.

"Brian, based on what you have said, I can only suggest that you speak with Harry about this after you are released back to LoCheVa."

Mila was still uncomfortable with the situation. She knew that even raising the rent could still mean trouble for her. She had one resident and a renter at the moment and she could have a second resident like Brian but at the moment her instincts said to have Brian go to a nursing home because of his chronic back pain and not being able to increase his pain medication dosage.

Brian looked at Mila and said, "Mila, my back pain will go away and it's only temporary. The medication the doctor gave me will work."

Mila realized that if Brian promised her that he would not try killing himself again she would be okay. Mila took Brian's word and trusted the doctor's advice.

"Ok" she said.

The doctor nodded and said, "We will see you tomorrow around 8am to pick up Brian and release him."

Mila nodded and Brian smiled. "Ok. I will see you tomorrow Brian. Be good."

Harry begrudgingly nodded and frowned then grabbed his jacket, and left the room and headed to the elevator and off to work. It was a Friday morning and Harry had a lot to get done that day before the weekend. He found his way to the elevator and pressed the button to go down to the ground floor. It was just past 8AM and he had a lot of work to do that day being the end of the week. He would get back to Brian, Mila and Dr. Halston later in the afternoon.

As soon as Harry had left Doctor Halston looked at Mila and then at Brian and asked, "Are you sure Brian this is what you

THE APPELLANT

want to do? Harry is your guardian and maybe should discuss it further." Both Doctor Halston and Mila knew Brian was going to need more help. Mila needed to get going as well because she had other patients to take care of that morning.

Brian and the doctor stayed in the room as Mila walked out and down the hallway. She needed to contact Harry and document the discussion as soon as she got back to LoCheVa. She reached for her phone as she approached the elevator and texted Pia and said she was on her way and that Brian was going to be released and returned tomorrow.

The elevator door was already open and she walked in and pressed the ground floor button and the doors closed and caught her breath. She looked at her face in the reflection of the elevator doors and she looked tired. She knew that the day had started off all wrong and that it was not over. She texted Harry to let him know of Brian's status as the elevated binged when the ground floor was reached.

Mila walked over to the ER nursing station and asked the same nurse if Brian was going to be in the same room tomorrow when she returned to pick him up when he was released. The nurse looked at her monitor and typed a few keystrokes and looked up and told Mila that Brian would be at that room for the rest of the day and through the night.

Mila asked, "I have a quick question. Has Brian been here before?"

"Yes, many times." The nurse replied.

"For what" Mila quickly interjected.

"He has come in here several times for accidentally falling. Let me take a look. Umm…He has been here at least 9 times in the past year."

Mila was startled. She had no idea that Brian had this history and Harry had not said something at the very beginning. She knew she needed to get with Harry right away and figure out what was going to happen with Brian and if his slips and falls were just a series of coincidences at the nursing home he was at, or was it something else.

The plot was thickening for Mila & LoCheVa's safety. This drama was getting to be too much too fast.

THE APPELLANT

Chapter 6 - Mila Confronts Harry

Harry was already at work when he received the text from Mila that she was leaving the hospital and that she needed to talk. Harry replied back to her that this afternoon would be fine sometime after 3PM.

Mila had returned to LoCheVa and helped Pia with their regular duties taking care of cooking, cleaning and help Joseph with his needs. Jane was doing some tidying up in her room when Mila came in.

"Hey Pia, I'm back"

"Hi Tita, are you ok?"

"Yes, Brian will be back tomorrow."

"Oh good, come give me a hand."

Pia was happy to hear that Brian was returning and continued what she was doing in the kitchen and could see Mila setting down her purse and keys.

The rest of the morning past quickly and 3PM came along. Harry texted Mila and said he was on his way. Mila replied to his text and said she was ready to see him and discuss what next was going to happen.

About 30 minutes passed and Harry pulled up in the driveway. He climbed out and walked up, knocked and made his way in to the living room to find Joseph and Jane sitting there watching some television and sipping on some tea.

"Mila?" he called out.

"I'll be right there." Mila yelled as she came out of her bedroom office from down the hall. She had been organizing her notes and logs regarding Brian's incident. She saw Brian standing in the living room and walked in to join him.

"Let's chat" she said.

"Ok. Have you heard from Brian or the doctor?"

"No, I left Brian and he was going to get some rest. I will go get him in the morning."

Harry and Mila started to discuss Brian's situation and Harry was definitely not feeling good about things. He did not want Brian to return to LoCheVa and he definitely did not like what Mila was offering.

Harry started out, "I don't want Brian to stay here because I am concerned he won't get the care he needs and besides it is too expensive."

Harry's internal thoughts included he did not like that Brian wanted to sell his house and if he did Harry wanted to be the beneficiary.

Mila countered, "Harry, Brian says he wants to come back and he needs good care. I can tell he likes it here rather than at the hospital or nursing home. Even the doctor agrees with him and me."

"Mila, you are a nice person. That is why we moved Brian here and I get it. He likes your care even though he has only been here a week. Anything is better than a nursing home."

THE APPELLANT

"Well then, why not let him come back. We can figure out how he is going to pay the difference."

"I don't want Brian to sell his house." Harry adamantly replied still gyrating internally about his own intentions.

Mila did not know what to say except to let Harry have his way and wait for Brian to return from the hospital.

"Fine - I will pick up Brian and bring him back tomorrow and you can tell him."

"Ok. I will be here tomorrow when you get back with him"

"That's fine. If there is a delay or problem, I will let you know"

Harry and Mila agreed to disagree and Harry departed without as much as a word to anyone else. In one way Mila was relieved because the hassle was becoming more than she cared for and it was putting her business at risk.

The rest of the day ended quietly with Pia and Mila taking care of Joseph and Jane and tending to their daily weekend activities. Mila had gone to Brian's room and got some of his clothes to take with her the next day because she knew he would not have anything but his pajamas that he wore to the hospital in the ambulance. She cleaned up his bathroom and made his bed comfortable and ready for his return.

It was Sunday morning and Mila returned to St. Catholic's to get Brian. She entered the hospital through the main entrance, and checked in at the nursing station. She was notified Brian was ready to go, and she went to Brian's room. When she got there he was waiting there in his gown. Mila had in her arms the set of his clothes to change into. He was happy to see her and also the clothes.

"Good morning Mila!" Brian said with such cheer.

"Good morning Brian. How are you? I have some clothes for you" as she walked in.

"Oh good - I did not like wearing my pajamas back home and the gown they gave me was so thin and cold."

"Did the doctor come by already?"

"Yes, he was in here about an hour ago right after breakfast." His back had bothered him through the night and the medication he got was good to take care of him for the day. The doctor had verified his prescription and made sure his refill orders were up to date.

"Did he give you any specific instructions?"

"No, none; just don't do that again." He chuckled.

Mila went over and helped Brian out of bed and handed him his clothes. He slowly changed right there not really caring what Mila saw. He was too old to care. Within a few minutes he was changed and ready to go. They both looked around the room and headed out to the nurse station. The nurse had Brian sign off on his release paperwork before leaving. He was happy to get out of there.

The drive back to LoCheVa was pleasant. Brian and Mila chit chatted about the weather and Brian enjoyed looking around and getting out. It took only fifteen minutes to get back and they parked

THE APPELLANT

in the driveway. Brian was able to ease himself out of the car and walked up to the front and Mila opened the door for him.

Inside Pia was cooking up something that made the whole house smell wonderful. Brian could tell he was home. Inside the living room was warm and everything was decorated so nicely and the couch and chairs looked comfy. He made his way back to his bedroom while Mila went to her bedroom and office and put away Brian's paperwork and made a note in her log.

When she came back out of her office she texted Harry and let him know Brian was back and getting settled in. About a half an hour passed before Harry replied and he was going to be coming over around 11am. Mila replied that would be fine. Lunch would be ready and he could join the rest of everyone for something to eat.

When Harry arrived, lunch was being served and everyone was in the dining room sitting down to enjoy a savory breakfast of sorts. Everyone got something to eat, and things seemed to be going well. Mila and Harry looked at each other and knew the time had come to discuss next steps.

"Brian" Harry said. "Let's go into you bedroom and discuss some things."

"Sure Harry. Mila, can you join us?"

Mila got up and she put away some of the dishes while Harry and Brian went down the hallway and into his room. Mila was right behind them. There was enough room for everyone to get comfortable sitting down. They did not have to close the door. They had plenty of privacy. The house was big and the rooms were very private and separated.

Harry started, "Brian, we need to figure out what we are going to do."

"What do you mean?"

"I mean, you cannot stay here."

"What are you talking about Harry?"

Mila just looked at Harry and Brian and did not say anything at first. She realized that she too wanted Brian to leave but she knew he needed better care than what he was received.

"I want to stay here Harry. It's not your decision."

"You don't have enough money per month in your retirement to cover the increase."

"That's nonsense. I am going to sell my home. I have no kids, and I don't need it anymore."

Harry was not happy about that. Brian had a very nice home in Hidden Valley and knew it would fetch a very nice sales price. Yet, Harry was his guardian and had to help Brian make good decisions if he was not able to do so. In this case, Brian knew what he was doing and did not agree with Harry.

Mila interjected, "Brian, I like you here and I am so happy to help you. You definitely need it, yet I am not sure this is the best idea."

Harry popped off in the midst of Mila's statement, "Brian, I don't agree. If you make that decision, I don't see how else I should remain your guardian if you don't listen to me."

THE APPELLANT

"Fine Harry - I can find someone else. Mila! She could be my guardian."

Mila's eye opened up wide and she knew that was not a good idea. She did not want to directly into conflict between the two of them and Brian's guardianship and finances. Yet Brian was determined.

"Harry, I have only been here one week, and I have had the best care ever. They have fed me, helped me with getting up and around, taking a shower, helping me with changing my clothes! Heck, when I was your neighbor at my home, you would not even bring me any food when I could not get it for myself. You would not even help me with getting around! What kind of guardian is that?!"

Brian was hot. He knew Harry was not going to fight him on this but Harry was not in the mood either. Harry shook his head and blurted out, "If that is the way you feel, then it's either Mila or Me? If you choose Mila and stay here, I am gone! Take me off as your guardian now!"

Mila was not sure what to say next. She just looked at Brian and Harry. Harry was not amused and just got up and looked at Brian and walked out. Brian looked at Mila and shook his head sideways knowing how Harry was, totally impossible to understand. All Brian wanted to do was stay at LoCheVa.

Mila got up walked out and Harry kept walking straight out the front door, and the screen door slammed behind him. Joseph and Jane were in the dining room and looked in dismay. Mila told them everything was okay and returned to Brian.

"Mila, I want you to be my guardian and I want to stay here."

She sighed and looked at Brian and replied, "Brian, this is just too soon. I want to help you, but Harry is super mad. I don't want to get between you two."

"Don't worry about Harry. All he wants is my money and my home. He will be fine. He gets like this."

Mila realized that no matter what she did at this moment, she needed to keep things sorted out and proper. Her business was thriving and she knew that this kind of argument could only cause problems she did not want and could not afford. Yet her heart was big, too big and her instincts said to stop. Yet she relented.

"Ok Brian, if you say so. Let's get you comfortable."

With that Mila finished picking up some of his things in his room and checked the bathroom to make sure things were clean and orderly for Brian. She did not want to bring up anything more that day regarding Harry's visit.

THE APPELLANT

Chapter 7 - Brian's Will

A few weeks passed and Harry had only made contact with Brian a few times. Mila and Pia were busy with their duties as usual. Mila had not brought up the guardianship discussion at all since the meeting with Harry after Brian was released from the hospital after his attempted overdose.

Brian's day and nights were quiet and his increased medication was holding him steady. His chronic back pain was always in the back of his mind. Mila was always there each and every day four to five times to help him with his movements around the house. Joseph and Jane were really starting to enjoy Brian's company too.

Time was passing nicely. Brian had not heard from Harry other than a regular call or check up to see if he was happy. Brian was happy and Mila was treating him very nicely as if he were family. Mila had a few care givers occasionally switch out with her when she had family commitments, and Brian was fine with that yet Brian really liked Mila more than the rest.

One of the fun things that Brian liked doing was when Mila would take him per his request and go down to Baldwin's Casino and do some gaming and get something to eat at the buffet, just a little bit of money spent, and watch the other patrons. Mila enjoyed taking him there aside from the smoky environment.

Finally, two months had passed and Brian asked Mila if she had a moment to go over some of his paperwork in his room. Mila checked with Pia and went on down the hall after making some notes in her logbook.

"Hi Brian, what can I do for you?"

"Mila, I have been thinking and I would like to make you my guardian and executor of my will."

Mila was not surprised based on the conversation from a few months prior and how Harry was barely even taking the time to check in on Brian she could understand his change of plans.

"Brian, I'm not sure that is a good idea."

"Mila, you are more than anything to me than anyone else I know or have left. Harry has all but abandoned me. Plus, I need to sell my house to I can pay you the rate increase you had mentioned was needed."

Mila pondered for a moment and considered the ramifications. If she were to agree, and she wanted to make sure Brian was taken care of, and she had given him a few months break from his rent increase, she would be willing do so on a few conditions. She needed to make sure his will and paperwork were done properly and Brian was sure of himself.

"If we do this, let's make sure your paperwork is done correctly and of course, you are sure of it."

"Absolutely" Brian replied.

"Then it's settled. Let me find a lawyer that can do this for you and have it done all legally."

Brian replied, "I have my lawyer that I used before. Let me contact him."

Mila said, "Sure.

THE APPELLANT

Brian seemed pleased and Mila was accepting of the fact since she had learned over the past few months there was really no one for Brian to reach out to. Brian's family was all gone, and he had no kids to leave anything.

The next day Brian tried to reach out to his lawyer and found out that his lawyer was out of town and would not be back for a month. Brian realized it was going to be something easy to update so he told Mila about his lawyer's status and he wanted things done soon so he figured another lawyer with a great reputation would work.

Mila and Brian set out the next day to find a lawyer that could do what Brian had described. It only took them a few days to find a local lawyer, a retired judge that was widely respected.

They made call to the lawyers office and explained their situation and an appointment was scheduled. It was going to be next week. The lawyer's office just asked to have existing wills and documentation faxed over which Mila provided per Brian. It was all set. They just had to relax and wait.

Chapter 8 – Paperwork Day

It was a Tuesday and Mila was getting things ready for Brian to go to the lawyer's office and make the necessary changes to his will. She had located with Brian's help the legal paperwork in his files and she made a copy what she had previously faxed to the lawyer.

"Good morning Brian"

"Good morning Mila."

"Are you ready to go?"

"Yep - Just give me a hand."

Mila went over and gave him a hand out of his bed and Brian had already got dressed into something simple for the meeting.

"When do you want to contact Harry about this change?"

"After we get things signed. He won't be happy but then again, I have not heard from him in quite a while."

As Brian continued to chitter-chatter, Mila picked up things around his room. Early she had completed cleaning the kitchen and living room from the previous day. She had updated her notes and logbook regarding Brian and Joseph's progress and status quo.

Mila had so many things going on between family and business one would be surprised that she could keep everything together and organized, yet she did.

The rest of LoCheVa was doing well in general yet a few residents were having a few normal aging issues but that was to be expected.

THE APPELLANT

Joseph was not doing very well, and Brian was staying well-kept and his appetite remained good. Jane on the other hand had only a few basic things going on. She had wanted to paint her room of which as renter she could do that without much of an issue. It was spring coming into summer so the paint fumes would not be much of a big deal. She got the idea from Pia who was in the midst of considering a change of colors in the bathrooms and kitchen.

As Mila continued to listen to Brian talk she was going through other priorities as well and making sure everything was covered. Brian ended his chatting and they both made their way to the car and got loaded and off they went.

On the way, Mila brought up the details of what can be done and Brian was happy to hear that Mila was going to be his guardian. Harry would not be happy with the news but Brian really did not care at this moment. LoCheVa was his home now and the last two months had shown him that Mila and Pia were the best.

Brian's back pain was still there yet his medication was keeping him satisfied. It had been months since his overdose experience. His agreement to pay more per month would be taken care of with his home going up for sale and changing his guardianship was just a move that made sense to him.

Harry was at work. The last time he had spoken to Brian was a week prior. He knew Brian was in good care though he did not want Brian to sell his home. He also wanted Brian to go into a nursing home instead of staying with Mila, yet what could he do. Harry knew Brian was happy and being taken care of.

Mila and Brian with all things considered were ready to go see Brian's lawyer regarding the guardianship changes. His name was

Judge John Smith. He was a retired judge and lawyer who had lots of experience with guardianship procedures. It was early in the day and the drive over to judge's office was short.

When they arrived, John was in his office finishing up on another client. He had retired from the bench after some twenty years of family court and law and he just wanted to continue his service in private practice. His family was happily taken care of and growing well. He was glad to have made their company.

His receptionist greeted Mila and Brian and asked them if they needed anything to drink. They both declined. She said the files Mila had faxed over they had and been processed. There were no issues that she could see. She pointed to the two chairs and as soon as they were about to sit John came out and spoke to both of them and shook their hands and asked them to step into his office. After a few minutes of introduction, he asked Mila to excuse them both so he could interview Brian regarding his changes. John said he would take a few hours and Mila did not object and said she would return in a few hours after running some errands. Mila departed. Bob and Brian then moved to the judge's office and sat down.

John asked, "Brian, why do you want to change your guardianship and executor?"

Brian started out, "Over the last few months, I have found that Mila is as close to family to me as anything. My neighbor Harry has been my guardian for a while yet he has not been treating me right and arguing with me regarding any of my decisions."

"Oh, I see." John replied. "Do you have family or any relatives?"

THE APPELLANT

"None" Brian shook his head and looked at the judge and made a nice smile to let him know that he was a happy man. Over the next hour John asked Brian a lot of questions about his home, his estate, what had happened over the last few years, and how he came to be in LoCheVa's care.

Judge Smith was a very ethical and sound judge and lawyer and his review was like any other guardianship case. There was going to be some that are unhappy and others that are okay with the outcome. In his case, Mila is what Brian wanted to be his guardian and executor and that would be the outcome of the judge's interview and recommendation.

Mila returned about 11:30AM. She had dropped him off around 10AM. As she walked in the receptionist greeted her again.

"The judge is just finishing up with Brian. He will be right out."

"Thank you" Mila replied. "May I wait out here?"

"Please, have a seat. Brian is almost done. The paperwork is almost ready. We just need to get some signatures."

Mila thought this was quite easy. She sat down and waited patiently. Her morning was quite busy with everything going on. Brian was going to be much happier in the long run.

John opened the door and leaned out, "Mila, would you like to join us. I have a few questions."

Mila got up and joined Brian who had just finished a grueling hour of questions and answers with John and though he looked a little tired, he smiled when Mila entered the room.

"Mila, Brian and I have concluded that you would be the best guardian for him. Do you have any issues with that?"

The judge surveyed her answer and gauged her response accordingly. He wanted to see her reaction, as if it were a question or a statement.

Mila replied, "As long Brian is ok with that. I only want to give him what is best."

John added, "Brian is pretty clear about what he wants and I don't see anything out the ordinary."

Brian commented, "Thank you John. I know it might seem strange for some, but Mila has been there for me and Harry is just too busy and he argued with me all the time before I came under Mila's care."

John seemed satisfied. "Very well then, I am just printing up the change of guardianship. Both of your signatures are required and my receptionist can sign as witness. Nothing is changing from the original will and guardianship except removing Harry and adding Mila."

Brian was pleased and he looked at Mila and smiled and clasped her hand and told her everything was going to be fine. Mila smiled back and wondered still if that was the right thing, but it was Brian's wishes and she had no reason to deny him. He had hardly anything left except to be happy.

John looked at their paperwork and they both agreed, and then stepped out to the reception area where his receptionist both notarized and witnessed the signatures. It was done.

THE APPELLANT

Mila and Brian drove home quietly happy. They knew they needed to let Harry know since he was still watching Brian's home and at this point knew it was going to be put up for sale. Once they got back to LoCheVa they both settled down and joined the others for an afternoon bite to eat and some tea.

Brian was super happy. Joseph, Jane and Pia were all glad to see some brightness out of him that was out of the ordinary. It was getting dinner time and they were all gathered in the dining room when Brian shared the good news.

"Everyone, I want you to know that I have asked Mila to be my guardian. Today we signed the paperwork."

Everyone looked at him with surprise.

"That's great" said Joseph.

"That's wonderful" said Jane.

Pia was happy to and congratulated Mila like usual. She had known what was going on over the past several months and did not fuss about things that made Brian happy. She knew he was in safe and better hands than Harry.

The dinner went along happily and everyone got themselves filled with some tasty entrees that Pia and Mila had been preparing over the past few days. The end of the day was coming and everyone retired to the living room and then prepared for sleep in their rooms.

MILAGROS RAYRAY

Chapter 9 – Informing Harry

The next morning Brian awoke and he felt pretty good. Mila was going by his room and looked in and he smiled. She said good morning to him, and she said today was a good day to let Harry know of the guardianship changes. Brian was not pleased with having to let Harry know but he had to.

"Can you get me the telephone?" Brian asked.

"Sure. Do you need Harry's number?"

"No. I have it memorized."

Mila handed him the telephone and he dialed Harry's number. It was early enough to catch Harry at home and not ready for work. The phone rang and rang and then he heard Harry pickup.

"Hello"

"Hi Harry, how are you?"

"I'm good Brian. What's up?"

"Harry, I have some good news. I have been thinking and I realize you have been super busy and helping me all the time has been a hassle. So, I decided to change guardianship these last few weeks."

"What!!" Harry exclaimed.

"Harry, now don't get mad."

"Why would you do that without talking with me?"

THE APPELLANT

"I knew you would be mad so why would I? You always disagree with me anyhow."

"Well then, who is your guardian now?

"Mila"

Harry paused on the telephone and narrowed his eyes and focus on the situation. What was going on? The last time he talked to Harry about a month ago after three months of care, he knew Brian was doing okay, but not to the point where guardianship would change.

"When did this happen?"

"Yesterday, and it's been planned for three weeks and we just signed the paperwork."

"I really wish you had not done that."

"Harry, you have been a good neighbor and friend but Mila is really more caring and I want her to be my guardian."

With those words, Harry knew that included mostly everything in Brian's will would probably now go to Mila. His forehead started to cringe and he started to glare through the phone. Brian could sense Harry's pause and disagreement.

"Fine, if that is what you want!" Harry blurted out.

Brian could hear Harry's anger and did not say anything. Harry just hung up at that moment. Brian heard nothing but dial tone and thought that was strange and went smoother than he had contemplated.

Mila looked over at Brian after the call and she noticed the look on his face.

"Are you ok?"

"Yes Mila. Harry was not too happy. I expected that."

"Will there be any problems?"

"I don't think so. Thank you though."

They both ended up getting ready and going for the day. Mila realized that Harry might not be very happy but what could they both do. Mila and Brian were both looking forward to a quiet week of activities. Harry on the other hand had ideas of his own and it was not good.

THE APPELLANT

Chapter 10 – Things Settle Down, Sort of

A few weeks had passed since Brian had informed Harry about the change in guardianship. Brian was very happy with his changes. The legal paperwork was filed and he received confirmation a few weeks later. His next step was to sell his home.

"Good morning Mila" Brian said as she walked by his room. It was about 7am and she was checking on everyone for the morning as breakfast was just about ready. Everyone was up early as usual making something special since the holidays were approaching and they needed something tasty to brighten their spirits.

"Good morning Brian" Mila replied as she came back to his door and looked in. She was dressed conservatively and ready for the day. She smiled and looked at him and then the window to see the birds outside were chirping and flying around getting their morning breakfast as well. She continued into his room and picked up a saucer, cup and glass from his previous evening and night. His medication was taking care of his back pains like expected.

"How are you doing this morning?"

"I am feeling great Mila. Whatever you are cooking smells great."

"Oh, that is something special that I am putting together today. I am sure everyone is going to like it." She finished picking up things and looked in his bathroom and shower and all was tidy and clean. She smiled and left his room to return to the kitchen.

The weather outside was relatively warm and the lingering smells of good food coming from the kitchen were welcoming. Mila had walked to Jane and Joseph's rooms as well and checked on them and helped Joseph up and prepare for his day.

Brian needed a little more help since his bones and body were in his early 80's. His walking cane and walker were conveniently located next to his bed which helped on mornings when he was achier than other mornings. This morning was not the case and was able to get up slowly.

Back in the kitchen Pia and Mila were busy getting breakfast ready and setting out some plates and silverware in the dining room. Mila looked around the living room and had just checked all the bathrooms, went back to her room and office and logged the morning activities. Nothing out of the ordinary to report; everyone was feeling good and no overnight issues to report.

LoCheVa was neatly organized to keep anyone from running into any furniture and bruising themselves. Plus, everything was comfy and warm so no one had to worry about sitting down, getting up or having any aches or pains from long periods of enjoying a nap or watching a long movie in the living room.

"Good morning everyone" Joseph said as he came into the living room and walked over to the dining room table. "Yum - Everything smells great!"

Jane was not far behind him and she looked outside the living room windows to see if there was anything new going on outside. "Hi Mila and Pia, everything smells great."

Mila smiled and finished setting the table, and Pia was wrapping up the last few breakfast items and setting them to simmer and putting things on trays and plates for transfer to the dining table.

THE APPELLANT

Everyone was getting seated when the phone rang. Mila went over and answered, and it was Harry.

"Hello Harry." Mila answered.

"Hello Mila. I am concerned about Brian. I have not heard from him in a little while. Is he doing okay?" Harry was at his home in Hidden Valley looking out his front window looking at some real estate folks putting signs in the Brian's yard and driveway, and going in and out of his home taking pictures of the property.

"Yes, of course. Why do you ask?"

"Well, there are some people over here at his house putting in the yard Home for Sale signs."

"Oh, Yes Harry. Brian had told you he wanted to sell his home for quite some time, and he had it listed last week."

"Is Brian there? I want to speak with him."

"Sure, just a second" Mila replied.

Mila looked over at the dining table where Brian had sat down, and said "Brian, Harry is on the phone. He wants to talk to you about your home for sale."

Brian had heard the phone conversation when it started and really didn't want to talk to Harry. He looked at Mila and replied, "Tell Harry everything is fine and I really don't need to talk about anything."

Mila looked at Brian and passed along his comments. Harry's reply on the telephone was not very comforting to Mila nor was it rest assuring that Harry was not going to start some trouble.

"Ok Harry. I will let Brian know." Mila replied and hung up the telephone."

"What did he say?" Brian asked Mila.

"He was concerned about your home for sale."

"That's none of his business. That was decided months ago."

They both looked at each other and Mila tried to brush off the idea that Harry was going to stir up trouble. Brian was happy here at LoCheVa and she was happy to be his guardian but Harry was not going to let things be.

Over in Hidden Valley, the real estate company was finishing up their appraisal of Brian's home. The outdoor signage, the door lockbox, and their paperwork on the counter inside along with plenty of pictures taken for the listing were complete.

Harry next door was still staring out the window after he got off the telephone. He knew he needed to do something. He was mad about being removed as Brian's guardian and now he was not going to be part of any of Brian's will or trust.

THE APPELLANT

Chapter 11 – Doctor's Good Check up

It was summer and Mila and Pia were busy with their day and their residents and boarder were doing just fine. Brian had a few appointments with his doctor over the last year and his latest checkup appointment was today.

"Good morning Mila" Brian said as he wandered down the hallway to the kitchen to get something to drink after breakfast. He was feeling rather good. He had been feeling better over the last few months since his medication was perfectly adjusted for his chronic back pain and Mila had been getting him around to see the area since the weather was so nice.

"Good morning Brian." Mila replied. She had been taking care of her kids and running all sorts of family errands. Her kids were out of school and having summer fun with friends. Pia was busy too learning a lot from Mila about home residential care and how the business works.

"Are you ready to go see your doctor today?" Mila asked.

"Yep, I am sure am." Brian pleasantly commented and walked into the kitchen and got a glass from the cupboard and poured some juice. That tasted good for Brian. He loved fresh juice in the mornings.

"Okay, get ready and I'll take you in about a half hour. That will make us right on time."

He nodded and walked out of the kitchen and back down the hallway to his room. He finished his juice and looked at the birds chirping outside and the sun was shining down on the backyard when he checked out his room before heading to his doctor. He looked down at his bed and then over at the mirror and he looked pretty good for being 80 years old. He felt good.

Another 30 minutes passed and Mila had got her things together and gave Pia some last minute instructions for Joseph and also to see if Jane needed anything when they ran to the doctor's office.

Brian and Mila walked outside and it was warm enough to not wear a jacket. The doctor's office was downtown near St. Catholic's. It did not take long for them to get there. The traffic was light and Brian knew the way by heart.

The doctor's office was on the 2nd floor in the annex next to St. Catholic's. His doctor's name was Wilson, Dr. James Wilson. He was a general MD who had taken on Brian for the past few years. Mila found a good parking spot in the garage across the street and it did not take them long for them to park and walk to the office.

"Good morning" Brian said as he walked in the doctor's office and greeted the by the receptionist.

"Good morning Brian" The receptionist replied.

"Good morning" Mila said as well. "We have an appointment today."

The receptionist recognized Brian and nodded and asked them to have a seat. They were on time.

"The doctor would be right you."

THE APPELLANT

They waited for only ten minutes when the exam hallway door opened and a nurse spoke, "Brian?"

Brian got up and smiled and walked over and down the hall. Mila waited and flipped through a magazine and looked at her watch.

The nurse walked Brian over to some scales and weighed him, and then took his height and then asked him to follow her to an exam room. When they got there he took up a seat on the exam table and the nurse made some small talk and then took his temperature and blood pressure.

"Perfect" she said, "You are in good condition."

Brian was happy to hear that. The nurse left him and closed the door. It only took a few more minutes after she left when the doctor came in.

"Hello Brian, how are you?"

"Great doc. couldn't feel better."

"How is your back? Are you still on the same medication?"

"Same meds, doing pretty good; the pain is still there but I have been doing much better. The warmer the weather the better I feel."

The doctor knew what he meant. Summer is better for most that have back and bone pain problems.

"That's good. I looked at your stats and chart and all seems good since we last looked at you; anything new?"

"Not really. Just moved into a residential care home and I like it much."

"Oh really" the Doc replied, "Where?"

"A placed called LoCheVa. Mila is the one who is taking care of me for the past few months."

"That's great. Did she bring you here today?"

"Yes, she is out in the waiting room."

"I'll have to meet her."

"You will like her." Brian finished.

"Well, as far as I can see, everything looks great."

Doctor Wilson continued his exam of Brian and looked in every nook and cranny and Brian looked to be fit at a fiddle and strong as an ox. When the doctor finished, they both got up and walked about and down the hall where Mila was patiently waiting.

When the door opened, Mila looked up and the doctor walked over to her and reached out his hand to shake hers.

"Mila, my name is Dr. Wilson. It is nice to meet you."

Mila got up and shook his hand replying, "Nice to meet you."

"Brian mentioned you were taking care of him, and I must admit he is doing great."

"I know. He had a few bad spots in the past few months, but he now he is doing good."

THE APPELLANT

"You are doing a fine job and he seems pleased."

Brian walked around the doctor and smiled at Mila and shook the doctor's hand and stood between them. The receptionist looked up for a moment and looked back to her work.

"Well, Mila keep up the great work and I'll see you in a few months."

"That's great doc. I am in good hands with Mila."

The doctor reached over and took a card from the receptionist that had the next appointment reminder on it and handed it to Brian, who in turn handed it to Mila.

"Well, I need to get back and to my next appointment. Have a good summer Brian."

Brian replied in thanks and Mila smiled too and they both left and headed back to the parking garage. That went well they both thought and headed back to the car.

It did not take long for them to get back to LoCheVa on Susanne Way and when they pulled up, everything was in bloom and Mila noticed the yard grass was starting to get a little long and needed to be mowed. Brian did not notice and he was happy to get back inside and relax until their late lunch.

Inside Pia welcomed them both back and Mila went to her bedroom and office and took the appointment reminder and put it on Brian's calendar. She felt like things were going well.

Nothing new had happened in a few weeks since Mila became the guardian and executor for Brian. Harry had pretty much been out of the picture since the last phone call. Brian's home had been on the market for a few weeks and a few people had called his realtor to inquire about his property.

Brian's home was highly valued and with the sale he was going to be able to pay LoCheVa their monthly rate with ease. It would not take too long before Brian had achieved his goals and was settled down once again, or was that the case? Things were about to get interesting.

THE APPELLANT

Chapter 12 – The State Gets Involved

The State had a large group of investigators and auditors for just about every individual and business activity under its watchful eye. Mila was very well aware of the state's power to make decisions to grant and deny her business activities. She was a very savvy business woman. To get her business license for LoCheVa, it was an arduous task that required lots of paperwork, background checks, and insurance and compliance requirements. She achieved those tasks diligently and timely.

Yet, ever since Brian's will and guardianship changes, Mila could sense something strange was going to happen with the State. For some reason she thought Brian was going to cause some risk or harm to her business but not by his fault. Again her instincts were to not have allowed him to return to LoCheVa after the suicide attempt yet again her big giving heart was in the way.

She realized that Harry was not happy either with the change of the will and guardianship. Though she sensed his anger and frustration at this point she could only continue on and keep taking care of Brian to the best of her ability. She realized if Harry had any problems he couldn't be further from the truth but that would not stop him from making a few calls and maybe cause some problems. Time would tell.

June 2006 and Mila and Pia were doing just fine. Joseph, Jane and Brian were all very happy. Mila's family and kids were happy busy with school and their lives. Nothing seemed out of the ordinary and then, "Ring, Ring, Ring"

The telephone in the kitchen rang. Pia was not too far from it and she picked up and answered.

"Hello."

"Hello" came from the other end. It was the Ombudsman office.

"Can I help you?"

"Yes, this is the Ombudsman office and we have an inquiry as to a Brian. Is he there?"

"Yes"

"May we speak to him?"

"Of course, just a sec"

Pia went down the hallway and she looked into Brian's room and he was sleeping. She looked at the clock on the wall and noted the time.

"He's sleeping. Can I have him call you back?"

"Yes, that would be fine."

Pia took the name and number and wrote it down and hung up. It was not too longer afterwards when Mila showed up after running errands and picking up groceries for LoCheVa.

Mila walked in and brought in some groceries and Pia greeted her like normal and that is when she gave Mila the message.

"Tita, a lady from the Ombudsman office called and wanted to talk to Brian."

THE APPELLANT

"Oh yeah" Mila replied. "What did they want?"

"They wanted to talk to Brian, yet he was asleep. I wrote their number and name on the logbook."

Mila looked around and finished unloading the groceries and looked at the logbook. Only 30 minutes had passed and it was early in the afternoon. So she picked up the telephone and called the number.

"Ombudsman Office, how may I direct your call?"

Mila said she had been called by their office and the receptionist directed the call. Within a few seconds Mila was talking with the person who had called and left the message.

"Hello, this is Amy."

"Hello Amy. This is Mila. You had called?"

"Yes, I was calling about Brian. He is one of your residents?"

"Yes"

"For how long"

"A little more than 6 months"

"Oh, I see."

"Mrs. RayRay, it has come to our attention that you have recently become Brian's executor of his will and his guardian."

"Yes, that is true."

"We are here to verify if that is proper."

"Of course it was proper. Brian is the one who wanted it done."

"Well, we need to check with Brian and since you are his guardian we needed to start with you."

Mila knew that this was going to be just the start of more questions. She was not stupid.

"That is fine. What can I answer for you?" Mila replied.

"We will have someone come out and visit with you and Brian soon and go over some basic questions. Okay?"

"That will be fine."

"Very good, and thank you for returning my call" Amy finished.

They both hung up the telephone.

A few days later, State Board of Licensure and Certification showed up at LoCheVa on Suzanne Way. The investigator asked to talk to Mila the owner of LoCheVa and they asked her several questions and concerns. Mila responded that everything was fine, and if they wanted to they could talk to Brian.

In the end they were satisfied with their findings yet still had concerns and questions.

Mila at this point knew something was definitely up. Was it Harry, was it just karma? She was not sure. She knew that for

THE APPELLANT

whatever reason, the state was listening to someone and obviously had its own agenda and protocol it was following.

She was ethical and very understanding yet for the life of her she could not understand why her generosity and good care was being questioned.

Another week passed and everything seemed fine and then the telephone rang. Pia was not there this time and Mila answered the phone. Pia was running errands for the Joseph and Brian.

"Hello" Mila said.

"Hello, this is Micah from the Ombudsman office. Is Brian there?" the lady on the other end of the telephone said.

"Yes. May I ask for what is the purpose of your call?"

"We are investigating a report regarding his will and guardianship status of his home for sale."

"Ok." Mila replied. She realized things were not going good, but what could she do. She was his guardian and his executor for his will, yet for whatever reason someone thought it was improper.

"I can get you for him."

"That would be great. Thank you."

Mila went down the hall to Brian's room and he was watching television and sipping on some orange juice.

"Hello Mila. How are you?" He looked up from his television show and set down his orange juice.

"It's the state Ombudsman office asking about your home."

"What do they want?"

"To talk to you"

"Ok. Let me talk to them"

Mila handed Brian the telephone and he answered he was indeed Brian and the ombudsman investigator asked him a few questions. He frowned a little and then replied.

"That is my home, and yes it is for sale. No, it was my idea and I don't need it anymore."

Micah the investigator was asking him the motivation for his sale, and he was simply telling her the truth. He wanted to sell it and did not need it anymore. He was happy living at LoCheVa and with Mila taking care of him.

"Brian, it has come to our attention that you might not be making this decision on your own." Micah said to Brian.

"Miss, you don't understand. I like living here and selling my home is my idea. I was not coerced or convinced to do so. It will help pay for my monthly care, that is all."

With that being said, Mila was listening as she should to make sure if there were questions for her, she could help answer.

"Thank you Miss. I appreciate your call. All is in order."

Only a few more seconds passed, and Brian looked at Mila and smiled and hung up. The rest of the day went uneventful.

Mila and Pia talked in the evening about the phone calls and the investigation and made sure that no matter what they would keep

THE APPELLANT

good logs and make sure everything they were doing was prepared for unexpected auditors and investigators. They loved their work and serving their patients yet the state was going to do their job too and see if anything was improper or wrong.

To Mila, this was the beginning of a long process that she was not sure she was prepared for. She would have to relax and just do the very best she knew how.

MILAGROS RAYRAY

Chapter 13 – The Slip & Fall Accident

It was now August 2006 and LoCheVa was running smoothly. Brian was doing just fine and Joseph and Jane were happy as can be. Pia and Mila were tending to their daily activities.

Brian was in the living room during the morning and had just finished watching a movie when he decided to step away and take an afternoon nap. He wandered down the hallway to his room and made his way to his bed. He climbed in and laid down for what seemed to him like an hour. His medication he had taken early in the morning was doing its job and he was feeling just fine.

About 4:30PM he had awoken and decided to use the toilet. He was use to this chore at least four times a day. Thank goodness his bladder was doing just fine. He ended up taking his normal time in the bathroom and decided to stand up and for some reason he lost his balance on his right side and fell down. A large thud came out of the bathroom and Mila heard it from the living room.

"Brian! Are you okay?" Mila called out and started to walk to Brian's room.

"Yeah, Yeah - I just slipped. Darn old legs." Brian exclaimed. Mila was just around the corner when she came in and found him there getting up from the floor. He grinned and frowned at the same time. He felt embarrassed but realized getting old is normally no fun at all.

When Mila walked into the bathroom, Brian was just getting up and she rushed to him and helped him up.

"Are you sure you are okay? Did you hurt yourself?"

THE APPELLANT

"No. I just hurt my pride. Nothing more" Brian replied.

"Here, let's get you over to your bed. Are you sure?"

"No, I am just fine. I just slipped. It's happened before."

Mila was concerned but knew Brian was very well aware of his situation. So she thought, okay, and helped him to his bed where Brian crawled in and laid down. For the rest of the day Brian rested.

Mila went back into the kitchen and talked with Pia and they agreed to make a note of his slip and fall in their logs. They finished making dinner and prepared the dining room table. It was about 6PM when they were ready for dinner.

"Joseph, Jane, Brian – time for dinner!" Pia spoke out loudly.

"Coming" said Jane.

"Coming" said Joseph.

"On my way" said Brian.

Each of the three made their way out and down the hallway to the dining room table. Mila had already set the table and each of them was happily seeing what was in store for dinner.

When Brian went to sit down, he made a little wince and Mila asked, "Are you okay Brian? Is that from earlier?"

"No Mila. I am just getting old." Brian replied and chuckled.

Everyone was seated and started to get themselves food from the several dishes that Pia had brought out. Everything looked so good and scrumptious.

After a half hour, everyone was full and content and made their way into the living room to enjoy the evening news. Brian found his favorite chair and Joseph and Jane each took up a spot on the long couch.

By 8PM everyone decided it was time to retire to their rooms. The evening was upon LoCheVa and while it was still late summer and the weather outside was nice, each of them enjoyed retiring into their own rooms to get relaxed, wash their faces and brush their teeth and change into something comfortable to watch television until they were ready for sleep.

For Brian, he stayed up a little later than most now that his medication that he took was allowing him to not get too sleepy or drowsy.

Pia and Mila had finished cleaning everything up in the kitchen and living room and was making their rounds through the house and looking into the bathrooms to make sure everyone was set for the night.

"Goodnight Brian." Mila said as she walked past his room.

Brian looked up from the television and smiled and replied to Mila, "Goodnight. See you tomorrow."

With that being said, Mila went ahead and wrapped up her log notes in her bedroom. Pia was doing something similar as well. They both wished each other a good night sleep and to bed they went.

THE APPELLANT

The next morning came early. It was about 5AM when Mila got herself up and was running some errands for her kids before the residents at LoCheVa got up.

When she got back, Pia was already in the kitchen making breakfast and lunch items, and prepping items for dinner.

"Good morning" Mila said.

"Good morning" Pia replied.

"Is there anything special we need to do today?"

"No. Oh, don't forget Brian wants some help this morning with his shower."

"Oh, that's right."

Mila from time to time would help Brian in the shower just to get him in and out of it because his feet were sometimes cold or numb from the medication and low circulation.

"I'll be right back."

"Ok"

Mila headed down the hallway to Brian's room and peeked in and he was up and moving around picking up things, and she was just in time.

"Good morning Brian, are you ready for your shower?"

"Good morning Mila. Yes, that would be great."

Brian moved a few of his things and made his way to the shower and put some of his clothes to the side that he had pulled out earlier to change into. Mila walked up to him and held his arm as he made his way in through the bathroom door and to the shower stall.

"There you go. Now just go ahead and ease off your robe and I can hang it over here."

Mila reached over and as Brian pulled his robe to his side, she noticed his left hip and the bruise that was on it. She blinked her eyes twice and looked at it with concern.

"Brian? You have a bruise on your hip; when did you get that?"

Brian looked down to his left hip and replied, "I don't remember - it was not there yesterday."

Mila recalled yesterday afternoon when he slipped. This could be it, but the bruise was not hurting him.

"Does it hurt?"

"No. Well, we need to have that checked out.'

"Well, take me to the doctor."

"No, we can't do that. We need to call the paramedics and then they can take you right in without waiting?"

"Really?"

"Yes, instead of taking you to the ER or your doctor, we can have it looked at right away."

"Oh, I see. Very well."

THE APPELLANT

Mila walked down the hallway and got the cordless telephone and walked back to Brian's room, and then dialed 911.

"911. What's the nature of your emergency?"

"Hello, this is Mila RayRay at Suzanne Way. I have a patient named Brian who has slipped and fallen. We need an ambulance immediately."

"Yes Ma'am. Is he awake and conscious?"

"Yes, he just slipped and fallen."

"Okay ma'am. I'll dispatch an ambulance. Can you verify the age of the patient?"

"Yes, he is 82 years old. He slipped and fell in the shower."

"Is he bleeding or having any difficulty breathing?"

"No. We just need an ambulance."

"Ok ma'am. I have dispatched an ambulance to your location."

"Thank you."

Mila hung up and looked at Brian and he was concerned but he realized it was the right thing to do. He trusted Mila.

Within a few minutes, Mila and Pia could hear an ambulance in the distance. Pia came down the hall and told Mila that the ambulance had arrived.

"Please open the door for them" Mila asked Pia.

Pia did as Mila asked and the two paramedics came in and introduced themselves quickly and looked over Brian who was at this time sitting on his bed in his robe.

"Hello, my name is Mike. What is your name?"

"Brian."

"Brian, are you in pain anywhere?" Mike asked.

"No, I just have this bruise on my hip from yesterday afternoon when I slipped while going to the bathroom."

"Yesterday, what time?"

Brian replied, "About 4PM"

The paramedic looked down at the bruise on his left his and put his hands to the edge of it and pressed down lightly see if it were sensitive. Brian did not flinch or wince. The bruise looked dark, but not terrible.

"Okay Brian. It does not look too bad but we are going to have to get this x-rayed. Are you okay with that?"

"Yes, I am fine with that."

Within a few minutes the fire department rescue had shown up too. They quickly came in to see both the paramedics in the process of needing the gurney from their ambulance. The two fire department EMTs were able to help with getting the gurney into the living room and down the hallway to Brian's room.

THE APPELLANT

Once there they got Brian situated on the gurney and lay down with his upper torso prospered up. Within a few minutes he was strapped in and being wheeled out.

Pia looked at Mila.

"Do you want me to go with you?"

"No. Stay here and watch over Joseph and Jane. I will follow them and tell them what happened."

Mila grabbed her purse and keys, and followed the paramedics out of LoCheVa and she got in her car and as the ambulance was loaded with Brian, Mila was already behind the ambulance ready to follow them.

The fire department EMT came up to Mila's car window and told her that the ambulance was taking him to Northern Medical Center (NMC) which was east of Suzanne Way. Previously St. Catholic's was the where they had taken Brian when he attempted to OD, but this time, he was taken to NMC.

It only took a few minutes and the ambulance was down the street to Prater Way and then some twenty blocks east to NMC. Mila pulled up behind the ambulance as they paramedics unloaded Brian and moved him into the ER lobby and directly into an exam room. She parked and grabbed her purse and phone and walked to the ER nurses station.

"Hello. I am with the man who was just brought in."

"What is his name?" The ER desk receptionist asked.

"Brian." Mila replied.

"Oh, yes. I see him listed. Can you give me his information?" The front desk asked.

"Yes." Mila handed her his emergency information she now carried with her in case of such instances. All his pertinent medical information was listed including prescriptions and allergies.

"Thank you. Please have a seat."

Mila sat down in the ER waiting room. She could see a doctor and an RN were tending to Brian. The RN was from the admission desk and station. They were looking at his hip and going over the report. It did not take long until the doctor came out and asked for Mila.

"Mrs. RayRay?" The doctor looked at Mila.

"Yes."

"My name is Dr. Jackson. Brian is doing just fine. His bruise on his hip, how did that happen?"

"He slipped yesterday in the bathroom."

"Well, it's not too bad, but we are going to take some x-rays to see if there is anything broken. He told me what happened."

"I know. He said he was not hurting, but the bruise I noticed today."

"Yes, that bruised fast. It appears that is due to his medication anyhow."

"Yes the Coumadin probably. This is not the first time he has fallen."

THE APPELLANT

"Oh really: How many times?"

"At least 9 times from what I learned from St. Catholic's"

"That's a lot of times."

"Yes: too many times"

The doctor looked over at the exam room and said that his x-rays won't take long and informed Mila she could wait. She could see Brian being moved in his gurney out of ER and down the hall, most likely to the X-Ray department.

Mila decided to text Pia and let her know what was happening. Pia replied and said that all was okay at the residence.

It was not long before the doctor came back and let Mila know the x-rays were completed and it showed that he had a broken hip bone and would need to be admitted.

"Mila, Brian's x-ray showed a fracture in his left pelvic bone."

Mila was beside herself. She knew this could be serious. However; the doctor was not too worried because he was aware of slip and falls and the elderly. It was common and diagnosing a hip break did require an x-ray and since Brian had not experienced any pain he was not worried about the lapse in time, about 15 hours.

"How bad was it?" Mila asked.

"Not bad. But I am glad you called and had him brought in. We have seen worse."

"What's next?" Mila followed.

"We are going to admit him and get him casted so his pelvis can heal. It's not that bad. We are going to get him some medication to speed up his recovery."

"What can I do now?" Mila finally added.

"Just give us some time today to follow our protocol and you should be able to see him in an hour or so."

"Ok. I am going to go get some things for him from his room at our residence."

They both agreed and Dr. Jackson walked back into ER and followed up with the staff as Brian was already being moved to a room and setup for being admitted for his recovery. Mila went to the ER nurses station and left her contact information.

Pia was back at LoCheVa when she received a text from Mila to get some of Brian's things together so he could be comfortable for his stay while being treated. Pia quickly put some things together so Mila did not have to wait too long to come and get them.

Joseph and Jane at LoCheVa were concerned about Brian and asked Pia what his status was as they noticed her picking up some personal items from his bedroom.

"Pia, is Brian okay?"

"Yes, he fractured his hip and is going to be admitted and treated. He is going to be gone for a few days. Mila is coming to get some of his things to make him comfortable."

"Oh, can we do anything to help?"

THE APPELLANT

"No, thank you for asking" and Pia put Brian's items in an overnight bag and put it in the living room. Mila was only minutes away and would not take long.

Fifteen minutes later Mila pulled up to LoCheVa and parked. She came in and smiled at Pia and looked at the items she needed for Brian.

"He's going to be ok. The doctor said it was not too bad."

"Oh good: we were concerned."

"They are going to admit him and keep him until his hip is healed. It should be only few days or less."

Mila looked through the bag of things Pia had collected and noticed his prescription was not included.

"Can you get Brian's prescriptions from the kitchen?"

"Sure" Pia went and got Brian's prescriptions from the kitchen, and then went to his room and bathroom and got those too.

"Thank you." Mila thanked Pia.

"Do you need anything else?"

"No. I am going to go back and see what room Brian has been assigned."

Pia was fine and said she was going to take care of Joseph and Jane for lunch and dinner. Mila went to her room and updated her log book and notes. Slip and falls are common but handling them properly is just as important as any other issue encountered.

Back at Northern Medical Center, Brian was being assigned a room and admitted to the hospital. The x-rays were re-reviewed and Dr. Jackson was already preparing for Brian to get casted so that his hip would be immobilized.

The nursing station on the floor where Brian was being moved to had his records and was getting his files ready. In the background, the medical records department was pulling Brian's medical history from the medical exchange repository system and they noted his previous hospital visits and medical history.

It was 2pm when Mila returned to NMC. She parked and walked in to find out which room Brian was moved to. She approached the front desk receptionist.

"Good afternoon, may I help you?" The receptionist asked.

"Yes, may I ask which room Brian is in?"

"Are you family or a relative?"

"I am his caregiver and guardian."

"What is your name?"

"Mila RayRay"

The receptionist had pulled up Brian's admittance record and it showed Mila's name on the approved list.

"Yes, Mrs. RayRay. Brian is in room 402."

"Thank you."

Mila proceeded to the elevator and pressed the up button. She had Brian's things with her along with his medication. She was

THE APPELLANT

hoping he was there and that she could see him and find out how he was doing. The elevator door opened and she pressed 4 and the doors closed. A few minutes passed and the door opened and she looked and found the room locator on the wall. Room 402 was just around the corner.

Pia was preparing afternoon snacks for Joseph and Jane when the doorbell rang. She looked up and noticed the time and went and opened it. It was a lady dressed nicely wearing glasses and she had a leather business binder under her arm.

"Hello, may I help you?" Pia asked from behind the security screen door.

"Yes, my name is Cathy Johnson from the State Board of Certification and Licensure. Is Milagros RayRay here?"

"No, she is at the hospital. Can I help you?"

"Yes, I am looking to interview Brian. Is he here?"

"No, he is not here."

"Ok. Do you know when they will be back?"

"In a few hours or so" Pia replied.

"Very well, here is my card and could you please have Mrs. RayRay give me a call when she returns. Thank you."

The lady then left and went back to her car and pulled away from the curb. Pia went back to her desk and made a note and then texted Mila about the visit.

Mila was just walking up to Brian's room when she saw the text, and room 402's door was closed. She knocked and opened the door, and Brian was inside in his bed resting. He looked up as the door opened and smiled as Mila walked it.

"Mila, you made it."

"Hello Brian. I brought your things and your medication."

"Thank you. I just got here from x-ray."

"How do you feel?"

"I feel good. A little sore from being prodded and poked by the doctor and their nurses, but I feel good."

"Have you eaten?"

"Not yet. The doctor said I cannot eat until after I am casted."

"Is it bad?"

"No, the doctors said the facture does not require surgery. It is very slight, but I need to be immobilized for a week or so."

"Here are some of your clothes to make you comfortable, and your medication and prescriptions."

"Thank you. Dr. Jackson said he is going to add something to help my hip heal, an antibiotic that will help with the healing to avoid any infection, and not mess with my other medication."

"Good. What else can I do for you? Do you need an extra pillow?"

THE APPELLANT

"Yes, that would be great."

Mila went over to the closet and found another blanket and pillow and brought that Brian. That took care of him just perfectly.

"Good afternoon Brian." Dr. Jackson walked in and surprised both of them. "I see you are settled."

"Hello Doc." Brian replied

Dr. Jackson shook Mila's hand again and Brian's.

"The treatment is not going to be too serious and the fracture was minor. No surgery required."

"Oh good" Mila sighed.

"Good" Brian smiled.

"You are going to be here for a week or so just to make sure we keep you under observation while your hip heals."

Dr. Jackson looked at Brian's chart and his medication orders and nodded.

"Get some rest and I will see you tomorrow. A nurse will come by and check on you in a while."

Mila picked up a few things that were on the table and put them closer to Brian so he could easily reach them. She then took the bed remote and handed it to him so he could adjust the bed to his comfort.

"Don't forget to take your medication."

"I know. The nurse will help me stay on track."

"What can I get you?"

"Nothing right now but I would love some of your soup and vegetables." Brian chuckled after he said that.

"I can do that." Mila replied. "I will check with the nurse to make sure that is ok."

Mila finished checking the bathroom and put Brian's clothes and personal things on the table next to his bed.

"Ok. I am going to run a few errands and be back shortly."

Brian smiled and gave Mila a big hug. When Mila left she looked at her phone and looked at the text message from Pia and left the hospital and returned to LoCheVa right away to see what was needed.

Pia was down the hallway when Mila walked in.

"Hello Pia."

"Hello. A lady came from the state asking for you and Brian." Pia walked into the living room and greeted Mila.

"What did she want?"

"She just wanted to talk with you or Brian."

"Hmmm" Mila thought. "Did she leave a number?"

"Oh yes, here it is." Pia walked over to the kitchen counter and got Mila the business card that had the name and number of the lady who had stopped by.

THE APPELLANT

The card read Cathy Johnson, State Board of Certification and Licensure. It had her number and address on it. She was from Carson City. Mila walked over and picked up the telephone and dialed the number.

"This is Cathy Johnson, can I help you?"

"Yes, this is Milagros RayRay from LoCheVa Residential Care. You stopped by."

"Yes, I was there to ask you or Brian some questions. When can I meet with you and Brian?"

"You can meet with me at any time. Brian is currently at NMC."

"NMC?"

"Yes, Northern Medical Center."

"Why is he there?"

"He accidentally slipped and fell yesterday."

"I see. I will need to interview him."

"What is this about?" Mila asked.

"It's about a complaint."

"A complaint?" Mila asked. "From who? For what?"

"I am sorry, that is confidential. This is just an investigation and some questions need to be answered. I am the investigator in charge."

MILAGROS RAYRAY

Mila could feel the pressure mounting again. First the Ombudsman called and now the state. What was going on?

"Mrs. RayRay. Your cooperation is required." Cathy retorted. Cathy could feel the angst in Mila's voice and wanted to ensure Mila was not guilty of anything but definitely under a microscope at this very moment.

Mila did not respond. She just knew in her gut that this was not supposed to be happening. Why did she deserve this?

"I understand" Mila finally replied.

"Thank you for cooperation. I will be in touch." Cathy finally noted and hung up.

Mila hung up and looked around the living room and the kitchen and knew she was in a situation she did not want to be in and she predicted it. What was going on? She had done nothing wrong. To make matters worse, Brian was now taking up more time of her and she wanted to be a great caregiver to all of her residents yet she had so many things to take care of between her family and business.

Back in Carson City, Cathy in her office looked at the complaint cover letter along with the log notes on her desk, and the complaint file folder labeled LoCheVa filled with official forms and notes. She had done some early investigation of LoCheVa and noted the number of facilities that were operating. There had not been any complaints but the number of facilities owned and operated by Mrs. RayRay made Cathy wonder why the investigation had formally been requested.

THE APPELLANT

The formal official complaint concerning Brian was being shielded from her as well. It was a credible complaint and it came from a secret witness source. The investigation was going to be thorough Cathy thought. She had three existing investigations and this one was no different except that it was out of the ordinary. The complaint was complex and had many specific elements that required more investigation time than other basic complaints because this source came in from two official state organizations that were unnamed.

Cathy was unsure of the depth of the problem but she knew that she needed to remain open to what she was going to learn and observe. She closed the file and put it away for the day. She was going to have to schedule several visits to see Brian and get his testimony and version of complaint since it did not come from him, a relative or family member.

MILAGROS RAYRAY

Chapter 14 - The State Investigates Harshly

Mila was patiently working with Pia regarding Brian's needs. The days passed and Mila visited Brian three times per day every day and he was progressing nicely. Brian was happy as can be. Doctor Jackson was monitoring and reports showed Brian's healing progress.

Cathy at the State was continuing her case investigation. Little did she know but her findings were based on half-truths and perception, not reality. The Ombudsman office was simultaneously working with Cathy on the investigation. For Mila, this was something she did not know was going on.

The background story the State was finding was that the business LoCheVa was created by Milagros RayRay to help the elderly and serve them in the Godliest way they knew how; however, the accusations from other sources were stated differently. She was accused of abusing and exploiting an elderly man and who knows what else. The initial investigation was expanding and continued to be inconclusive and ongoing.

It was one week into Brian's stay at NMC when Mila came in to Brian's room and learned about something she did not expect.

"Good morning Brian" as Mila walked in like she had a couple times every day for the past week.

"Mila, a lady named Cathy came by yesterday afternoon after you had left and asked me a quite a lot of questions."

THE APPELLANT

Brian explained to Mila that the State had been there at least an hour asking him all sorts of questions about his home, his will, her as guardian, and how he came to stay at LoCheVa.

"Brian, did they tell you who was complaining?"

"No, except they were concerned about my home and why I was selling it. I told them why and it was my idea."

Brian shared with Mila his concern and told her that he was not happy with what he sensed was going on.

"I told them that you were the most kind, loving and caring person I know and have helped me so much."

"Brian, if they keep this up I don't know what they are going to do?"

"Mila, no matter what I will do whatever I can. I don't know why they are doing this to me and you."

"I don't know either. You are a wonderful person and I cannot understand why they are trying to find something to accuse me of doing."

To professionals in the senior care industry, slip and falls happened all the time especially to the elderly. Brian told the state investigators the absolute truth that LoCheVa and Mila had nothing to do with his slip and fall let alone his hip fracture yet their protocol and investigation was somehow being biased and influenced by an outside force. There was a hidden agenda. Who was controlling it?

For the next two weeks, Cathy from the Bureau of Licensure and Certification, and another investigator from

Ombudsman was visiting Brian and interviewing him daily gathering information about his condition. He was getting frustrated.

Mila visited Brian daily at the hospital and learning what he was experiencing and she could not understand why the harsh and aggressive nature of their investigation. Every day Brian while at Northern Medical Center was now being interrogated along with Mila at her home office at LoCheVa. Mila explained countless times she was doing everything ethically and it was Brian's will and wishes for the guardianship and change in his will, and the sale of his home.

The Bureau of Licensure and Certification was up to something trying to convince Brian to cooperate with them so they could twist the story and charge LoCheVa with Elderly Abuse and Neglect. The State continued interviewing Brian about his care, about his financial affairs. The State wanted to know if Mila from LoCheVa had been taking advantage of him financially and of course Brian continued his tireless resolve and response that she had nothing to do with his decision making.

Cathy on the other hand continued to investigate Brian whom she found as a very faithful and honest individual, yet she continued to pressure him because she believed he was hiding something. However, Brian was very generous and at the same time tough, strong with integrity and character and Cathy soon realized she could not put words in his mouth. All of Brian's activities the Bureau of Licensure and Certification learned about during the investigation probably led them to more and more questions for which they figured was just in their cause to bend the story against Mila and LoCheVa.

THE APPELLANT

Yet the State was now going beyond their scope and rightfully so, they were now overstepping their authority. The State had learned Brian loved to go to Baldwin's and play slot machines and eat lunch. For Brian he was nearing the end of his life and the need for a house was meaningless for he could stay at LoCheVa and receive great care and enjoy his remaining days without need of financial worry. The State had a different idea, opinion and agenda for Brian. Was the State overstepping their authority and boundaries in this case?

Mila soon realized that Brian's investigation was going to be the turning point of her life and career. Her life, her dreams, her hopes, and desires to take care of the elderly, and raise her family were slowly being shattered by the hands of a justice system being unjust.

Another week passed and Brian promised Mila that he would clear LoCheVa's name up to his last breath. It was a Sunday and Pia and Mila came into see Brian.

"Hello Brian" Mila and Pia said as they walked into his room.

"Hello Mila and Pia" Brian replied.

"Are you doing okay?" they asked.

"I feel pretty good. I am just so tired of the state asking so many questions about me and you."

"I know Brian. We are exhausted as well."

"What's going to happen to me?"

"You only have a few more days to finish your recovery and you should be able to come home."

"I really want to get back home to my room" Brian sighed with relief and then looked Mila in the eyes intently.

"You know you need to go get a lawyer and make sure it's a good one. I have idea and fear they are going to accuse you of something" Brian said as he was clearly emotionally choked up.

He continued, "I promise you Mila. No matter what I promise with my last breath I will clear your name."

"Hopefully it won't get to that" Mila sighed and half smiled with a concerned frown, and reached out and held his hand.

Trying to brighten his day Mila said, "We brought you some nice things to read and a little bit of home cooking, you know the things you like."

Brian returned a smile and tearful wink. They were thankful for the brief moment of some pleasantness. Mila and Pia stayed with Brian for another hour and after what seemed like a lifetime, they parted and hugged and went back to LoCheVa to take care of the others.

Over the next few days, Brian put together a statement saying that his fall was clearly an accident and that Mila was a very loving and caring person who would never do anything to hurt anyone. Brian had been very aware of what was going on, and the State probably thought he was not coherent and very aware of what was going on. He only asked Mila to get a solid lawyer to help defend them both. That would be a very smart decision. Mila did exactly

THE APPELLANT

that yet she was not fast enough to protect them both. The State was moving faster.

Mila found a lawyer through a friend who was a caregiver as well who had been accused of this type of charges yet Mila did not realize the result was a plea deal of guilt. Unfortunately for Mila the lawyers she was going to end up securing would change their minds and either drop her, or indicate an innocence plea was unobtainable for the lack of money she had.

In the end it did not matter to the State. For them it was merely another file and another investigation. An investigation team bent on goals with a lack of training and a well-oiled legal prosecution machine with unlimited resources and the ability to block and restrict anyone anywhere from doing anything other than their will.

To Mila and her legal defense, the letter Brian signed indicated Mila's innocence and his will and desire to have her continue his care and his desire to return to LoCheVa. They believed this would be sufficient regardless of the State's investigation methods and doctored reporting and twisting of facts and timelines, let alone a 3rd party with a hidden agenda against Brian and Mila.

Mila at the time did not know that the State and legal system would later deny the letter since it was not created by Brian by his own hand writing. It only contained his signature. It would be a significant blow to their legal defense.

Cathy at the State concluded the investigation had enough to charge LoCheVa of elderly abuse and neglect, and eventually exploitation. Her investigation though she believed complete with all the information she had gathered she did not know was very flawed.

She was going to make Brian's case look like normal, but it was not even close. Could she make Brian a ward of the State and begin to make decisions for him in order to achieve the objectives of the State? Based on her interviews all she could conclude is that the State's position was to protect him for his own good in their estimation of what was good and not what he wanted. That was the critical error in their agenda. Her next step was to close her investigation and hand it over to the system and let the system take over. Her three months' worth of work was going to be a feather in her cap and a gold star on her resume, one of the last things she would do before she retired. She was pleased.

It was September 2006, and the preliminary investigation of Brian 's case was closed. A secret witness was notified of the investigation status, and Cathy handed over her investigation findings to her boss, the Director of the Bureau of Licensure and Certification, Ashley Stern.

Mrs. Stern scheduled a visit to see Brian at NMC. When she went there she was greeted by Mila who was caring for Brian. Mila was in the room with Brian taking care of some of his needs when Mrs. Stern walked in.

"Hello, Brian?" as Mrs. Ashley Stern leaned in and opened the door to room 402.

"Yes" Brian said. "Come in."

Mila had stopped what she was doing and walked over to greet Ashley.

"Hello, my name is Ashley Stern of the State Board of Licensure and Certification. How are you doing Brian?"

THE APPELLANT

"I am doing well. I can't wait to get out of here."

"That's good." Mrs. Stern replied.

"Mrs. RayRay, are you aware of the situation?" Ashley asked.

"Yes, I am aware that Brian's slip and fall was an accident."

"Yes, I see. Well, it is more serious than that. Our investigation is almost complete, and I believe you might be charged with something."

Mila just stared at Ashley with a look of bewilderment. How could this be Mila pondered? Brian also had the same look on his face.

Brian butted in and said, "Mila did not do anything wrong. I was the one who slipped and fell."

"Yes, Brain, but you also did not get taken to the hospital immediately and get checked out."

"But I said I was fine. It was not until the next morning did I see the bruise. I felt no pain."

"Regardless Brian, the investigation has other items we are following up on. There is nothing to be done."

"Mrs. RayRay, please be aware that you may be charged shortly. That is all I can say. I just wanted to visit with you Brian and check in on you as well since Cathy my investigator has concluded her work."

Mrs. Stern excused herself from the room very quickly, abruptly leaving Mila and Brian there alone. Mila was frantically confused and not sure why this was happening.

"Brian, I am going to do whatever I can."

"Mila, you did nothing wrong. Please get us a lawyer to keep me from leaving here and going to a nursing home."

Brian pleaded and Mila could only hold his hand and then after a few moments, got her things together and left in search of an attorney and a good one for him.

After the unexpected meeting by the Mrs. Stern from the State with Brian and Mila, the Ombudsman office in conjunction with the Bureau of Licensure and Certification coordinated their investigation findings in order to shore up their cases against LoCheVa. The internal cross sharing of information was not to become public and remain sealed if their case was to prevail against LoCheVa.

At this very moment, Brian was alive and well and was ready to be discharged when to his surprise, the Bureau of Licensure and Certification intervened not to let him return to LoCheVa.

Brian was in his room when Cathy from the State arrived to inform him of what had been decided through the investigation.

"Hello Brian. How are you doing?" Cathy asked.

"I could be better. Are you done with your questions?" Brian arguably replied not feeling very good about the entire situation. Being eighty years old did not allow him much room for a sense of humor let alone any patience.

THE APPELLANT

"Am I ready to be ready to be released? I am ready to get out of here."

"Not exactly; I am here on behalf of the State to inform you that you are not going to be released and returned to LoCheVa. The formal investigation is now concluded and we have found that you are not able to continue there."

"What???!!!" Brian looked at her in surprise and confusion and almost absolute frustration.

"There's no way I am going to do that!"

"Brian, it's for your own good. We believe that you have been taken advantage of by LoCheVa and the State is taking over on your behalf to protect you."

"That makes no sense!" Brian roared back and leaned forward in his bed and went to get up.

"Brian, you are now a ward of the State. The guardianship has been revoked from Mrs. RayRay and your estate is now under our protection."

"But, you can't do that. Mila has done nothing wrong. Everything that has happened is my will."

Cathy was not there to debate with Brian. She was the messenger and she knew that the decision came from higher up.

"Get out, Get out now! I am going to talk to my lawyer"

"Brian your behavior is not going to help. You are considered unable to make your own decisions and as a ward of the State the decisions have been made."

MILAGROS RAYRAY

"Get out, get out again I say before I call the police!"

Cathy relinquished and without any more to say, leaving the room with a cold and impassionate stare. She did not leave any paperwork, nothing, just the empty sound of Brian's life and decision making stripped away from him.

Brian could not believe this was happening. His heart and mind was racing and he could not understand. He was open and honest with the State and this is what they did! He could not believe what had just happened. He was unhappy, angry and lost. Where was Mila? What had the State done to him and her?

The State was just getting started. They had enough gumption to begin charges against LoCheVa and Mila and leverage and twist Brian's testimony. The State was also being fed bad information from secret sources that had an axe to grind with Brian for changing his will, guardianship and other things like his home. Their motivation was to be no one's knowledge. Their motivation was revenge and retaliation and the State was being used as the hammer and nail to get that done.

What was about to happen next would accelerate the State's cause and agenda and was not going to be nice about it. Like a wild animal on a leash that was about to get released and let go and attack the innocent, this was the State's next agenda item – get Brian in their hands and tighten their grip around LoCheVa and strangle them both. Was this the real situation or just mere coincidence?

All Brian wanted was to live the rest of his life with Mila and LoCheVa and enjoy what little bit of his life he had. The State had a different agenda and it was over-reaching and like always, just following what they believed was best. Sometimes the government

THE APPELLANT

intercedes into one's constitutional rights and without conscience just executes rather than reasons. Brian was a reasonable man and Mila was helping with his end of times. Others had different agendas and that would prove itself in short order.

MILAGROS RAYRAY

Chapter 15 – Brian transferred against His will

It was September 2006 when the State took Brian as a ward to the Skilled Nursing Facility called Reno Living Care. LoCheVa was sent a mandate order from the State that they were not allowed to be in contact with Brian.

Brian had begged Mila to please hire a lawyer at whatever cost and he would reimburse LoCheVa, but at this very moment Brian did not have any more money because the State froze all of his assets.

At the same time Mila was being pressured by the Nevada Ombudsman for more information regarding her guardianship and involvement in Brian's will, and the listing of his home that Brian had just initiated a few weeks prior.

It was to no avail. Mila needed to get a lawyer for Brian's needs. She went and hired local Reno Attorney Warren Carlson and signed the contract and agreed upon whatever the cost maybe that LoCheVa would shoulder and handled all the costs on behalf of Brian per his wishes. Mila asked Mr. Carlson to make sure Brian was being taken care of.

Warren Carlson wasted no time and arranged to visit Brian at Reno Living Care. Upon Warren's arrival, Mila stayed in the car and waited, while he registered to the front desk and asked to speak with Brian. After being approved of the visit, Warren went to Brian's room and upon walking in found Brian unconscious. He tried to wake him several times but Brian was unresponsive. Was Brian heavily drugged? Why could Brian not be awoken? Warren waited

THE APPELLANT

for thirty more minutes and tried again but still Brian was unresponsive.

Mila knew that she needed Brian's testimony through her Attorney Warren Carlson in order to talk on her behalf and provide a written declaration and statement to clear LoCheVa's name.

Mila continued to wait outside for Warren to return and hand Mila a report or a statement from Brian. She was anxious and impatient, but it did not take long. Warren returned and Mila received a devastating disappointment that Brian was heavily drugged and Mr. Carlson was unable to wake him even after shaking him. The nurses said they had given him morphine to make him comfortable. How much morphine was Warren's concern; was it too much?

When Warren came back to the car, he advised Mila she was just wasting money because there was no way he would be able to talk or get a statement due to his condition. Mila informed him she would take that chance for him to go another time and another day. Mr. Carlson mentioned that he loved Mila's money but if they continued to drug him that would be the end of Brian's life.

So Mila decided that she needed talk to Doctor Carey Johnson, and let her know what had happened to Brian. Brian was fine after the fall and he was alive and well and now placed into a nursing home against his will, drugged and sedated, and in a place Brian despised. Brian had begged to return to LoCheVa and the wonderful care from Mila and Pia. That would never be as Mila soon found out.

MILAGROS RAYRAY

Chapter 16 – Mila Indicted & Charged

The morning started like normal. Mila had an idea something might happen today. With all the questions and calls from the state's licensing board and other government agencies, and the strangest of inquiries, she realized the State was already preparing to do something that she might not like. The street on Suzanne Way was quiet and the autumn season had begun. The leaves were starting to turn color and the birds and squirrels were busy gathering nuts and other forms of food, tucking and hiding things away in the trees and bushes.

Mila and Pia had tended to Joseph and Jane needs, and cleaned up things ready for an early dinner when she heard a knock at the front door. She put away some dishes and utensils then wiped her hands with a dish cloth and walked to the front door. She glanced into the mirror in the hallway to make sure her hair was neat and there was nothing out of place. She opened it and two very tall men in uniform were standing on the outside of the security screen door. They both looked serious and daunting in their dark uniforms.

The one officer on her left, she could see his name tag was Office Smith who asked "Are you Mrs. Milagros RayRay?"

"Yes, I am." Mila replied. She looked at the other officer and his name tag said Officer Jones. She was unsure of what they wanted yet she was use to unexpected visits from the State.

"My name is Officer Smith. I have warranty for your arrest. Please step out and turn around and put your hands behind you."

THE APPELLANT

Mila was in absolute shock. The look on her face was absolutely in fear. She knew there was trouble but enough to warrant an arrest.

Mila stammered, "What? What am I charged for?"

"We have an indictment and warrant for your arrest for elderly abuse and neglect."

One of the officers took her by the arm and turned her around and she started to resist but the other officer, Office Jones immediately gave her the Miranda Rights.

"You have the right to remain silent. All that you say can and will be held against you. You have the right to an attorney and if you cannot afford one, one will be provided for you. Do you understand these rights?"

"Yes." Mila replied. Mila was in shock and starting to shake.

Inside LoCheVa, one of her assistant caregivers and boyfriend named Alex was standing just inside and listening to what was happening. He was absolutely surprised as well. Mila while being handcuffed instructed Alex to contact Pia. She was not sure what was going to happen.

Mila yelled, "Alex, contact Pia. Have her bail me out!"

Alex nodded to Mila as the officers completed taking Mila into custody. Office Smith and Jones escorted Mila to the street and their police car and loaded her securely in the back seat, and then transferred her to Parr Boulevard, the county detention center where she would be processed for the charges. It all happened so fast that

MILAGROS RAYRAY

Alex did not know what to do next. The front door was open, and Mila had been taken away.

Alex had no choice but to react. Within a few minutes, Alex was on the phone talking to Pia who reacted by totally freaking out from Alex's description of what happened.

"What? Mila arrested?" Pia exclaimed over the phone.

"Yes, just now. She is being taken to Parr Boulevard."

Pia was at another LoCheVa residence and immediately packed her personal items and prepared to get Mila out on bail. She did not know how much that was going to be.

At the same time, Mila in the police car was arriving at Parr Boulevard and was driven through the processing gates. Mila did not know this but this was going to be a familiar site in the near future.

She was taken from the police car and taken inside and unhandcuffed and put into a holding cell. Her personal items like her watch, belt and other items were removed from her. The duty officers looked at her with disdain and even scowled while processing her in. Mila felt terrible.

"Milagros RayRay?"

"Yes"

"You are going to be here for the night. A judge is going to review your case and you will be arraigned. If all goes well, you will be released tomorrow."

"I have to stay here tonight?"

THE APPELLANT

"Mrs. RayRay, you need to understand. You are under arrest. You are allowed one phone call."

Mila was granted her one call and she called Pia to let her know what had happened. Pia had heard from Alex already and knew what to do. Pia and Mila were going to have to wait the night and await a decision from a judge in the morning.

Mila was scared and inside the Parr Boulevard detention center which was not very hospitable. She could only try to calm her fears. She was alone in a very foreign place and time seemed to stop and everything stood still. She looked around at the other prisoners in there. She was in a big open room. There was no rhyme or reason to the holding and detention area. They all were ordered her and there, then ordered to eat and then be quiet.

Mila did not sleep at all that night. She just lay down on her cot, curled up and scared. She did not eat. She closed her eyes but could not sleep. All she could hear was others snoring and stirring all through the night.

The morning came, and all the women were being called by name for various messages. Each was being called to a hearing room where each faced a video camera and a video screen where each would face a virtual judge on the viewing screen.

Mila's name came up and she approached the judge on the screen.

"Milagros RayRay. I have reviewed your case and have set your bail at $20,000. If you can make bond you will be released. You have one phone call. If you do not have any questions you are excused."

Mila had no questions and pulled away from the judge on the screen. She was then given the chance to walk to the phone in the hallway and when she did, she made one call. It was to Pia.

"Pia?"

Pia answered, "Yes. Are you okay?"

"No, are you crazy?"

"Well what do you want me to do?"

"I need to have you get $2000 and get my bail posted."

"Okay. Where do I go?"

"Just get $2000 cash and bring it up to Parr Blvd."

"Okay. I'll be right there."

Mila hung up and was escorted back to the holding area. Pia on the other hand immediately got in her car and went to the bank and withdrew $2000 cash and drove to Parr Boulevard where she quickly got Mila released.

In the car back from the Parr detention center Mila and Pia just sat there quietly and did not say a word. Mila was shaking and overtaken with fear and embarrassed. This was not supposed to happen. Brian promised me this would not happen.

When Mila and Pia pulled back into the driveway at LoCheVa they both went inside and tried to sort out what had just happened. Mila was emotionally in tears and being torn apart inside. She had not slept that night and all the sounds inside the detention center still rang out in her ears.

THE APPELLANT

On the other side of the valley, the District Attorney was busy getting charges pressed against Mila and LoCheVa for neglect, abuse and possibly exploitation. The patient was Brian. The patient who refused to say Mila had done anything wrong. Yet the state's investigation was red hot with conviction and blame. Their investigation was flawed and unfortunately the law says innocent until proven guilty and in most cases in this era one is treated as guilty until proven innocent. That was Mila's situation and it was unfolding rapidly.

Back across the valley in Sparks, Mila was utterly confused and needed to rest. She went back to her bedroom and office and lay down. Pia went to the kitchen and returned to tending to the daily tasks of getting the afternoon meals and evening dinner ready for Joseph and Jane.

A few hours passed and then the doorbell rang. Pia went and answered it. It was a police officer.

"Yes, may I help you?" Pia asked without opening the security screen door.

"My name is officer Fawcett with the County Sheriff's department. Are you Mrs. Milagros RayRay?" the officer asked.

"No, she is inside."

"Maybe I speak to her. She needs to sign for some papers."

Pia turned and leaving the door locked went and woke up Mila who looked rather tired and in shambles. Pia explained who was at the front door, and Mila got up and went into the living room and to the front door.

"Yes. I am Mila."

"My name is Officer Fawcett. I need your signature ma'am."

"For what?"

"You are being indicted by the District Attorney's office. You need to sign for these papers."

Mila swallowed really hard and opened the door and stepped out and signed the paperwork. The officer was alone and Mila could tell he was young and probably new to the force, and just stood quietly and did not say a word, just a nod and no other expression.

He gave her the documentation in a folder and said she was to appear in the next 45 days. Mila's heart was pounding heavy and she sighed and her eyes started to hurt from what was to come. She had known God before but at this moment she really needed some help.

The police officer excused himself and Mila slipped back inside the security door and closed it, and watched the officer return to the curb and police car. She got in and slowly pulled away. Mila looked down at a copy of the paperwork she just signed along with a yellow packet attached and felt her stomach start to hurt. Her residents were in their bedrooms resting or watching television or talking to a family member on the telephone.

Mila returned to the kitchen and looked at the packet and opened it. The top copy was from the County District's Attorney office indicating the charges, and a second page was from the State Department of Licensure from an Ashley Stern. Mila had spoken with Ashley a week prior about Brian. Mila had answered her questions very politely and correctly, and in no way did she think Ashley was going to be the one responsible for this moment. There must have been something else going on.

Mila walked over to the kitchen and picked up the telephone. She walked into her bedroom and office looked for Ashley's number. She found it after a few moments and called the State Department of Licensure to speak to Ashley Stern. Mila could hear the phone ring and ring and finally the state's automated answering system answered. Without listening to the message Mila pressed the extension number she had for Ashley and it rang through and Ashley picked up.

"Hello, this is Ashley may I help you."

"Hi Ashley, this is Mila RayRay from LoCheVa Residential. I am wondering if you are aware I was just charged by the County District Attorney with elderly abuse and exploitation? Are you aware of this?"

Ashley replied, "Mrs. RayRay. Yes I am aware and I cannot comment."

Mila was confused. "Are you saying you were aware of this and your office did not contact me or my company?"

"Mrs. RayRay, I am aware of the charges and unfortunately our office cannot comment on the charges. You need to seek legal advice."

With that comment from the state, Mila hung up and her worries just increased. She was getting mad. What was going on she wondered. She needed help and fast. Her mind and heart raced. She looked around the living room. Her thoughts were mixed.

The rest of the afternoon went slow and Mila reached out to her family and friends on her problems that were going to become a nightmare and one of them said they knew of a few lawyers who was perfect for this kind of situation and has defended against this problem before. What happened next was earth shattering to Mila.

Before Mila's trial, she had to make sure she hired the best of the best lawyers in the area since her life was at stake. Mila's research went on for a few days to find out which lawyer would be perfect or the best lawyer who can defend her specifically for this kind of case.

The lawyer that she found was Ethen Daniels. Mila was not sure he would be the perfect lawyer for her defense but she had to trust someone. Daniels had helped an acquaintance of Mila's with a similar case and she hoped he would get everything sorted out.

THE APPELLANT

Chapter 17 – Brian Dies in State Custody

It was early November 2006, and Mila needed to get some information from the doctors and those who had last seen Brian, taken care of him, and those listed as medical attendees of Brian. The information she was collecting was going to help her case and help fill in any gaps that State had against her that was wrong.

Mila was at NMC waiting to talk to Doctor Carey Johnson when Mila's lawyer Ethen called her to let her know that Brian had died. He was found dead November 8, 2006 from an apparent heart attack. Ethen said to not even bother talking to Doctor Carey Johnson right now. As her lawyer, Ethen Daniels instructed Mila to go straight to his office figure out what to do. The most valuable witness, the most credible person who witnessed everything and knows what really happened was dead.

Mila's mind raced with questions. Here she was in the middle of an indictment and the only witness to speak the truth is now dead. How did he die? How was this possible? Was there a documentation or statements that the State or County DA had obtained that could help Mila's side of her innocence? Would the State or County DA hide that evidence? She could not even reach the medical staff to find out the truth. Could she be charged with manslaughter? She had no idea how fast her world was spinning out of control.

These questions repeated through Mila's mind as she drove to her lawyer's office. Brian was gone. That is all she thought. At that moment Mila felt like it was the end of the world for her, the only person who can and willing to testify a on her behalf was dead.

She knew for a fact that they killed him for a lot of reasons.

1). He was the only one who knows what kind a person she was and how grateful he was and she was for such excellent care

2) Brian was going to be able to testify against the State or County DA and to argue why his rights had been stripped away against his will while he was coherent

3) Brian was willing to stand up for what is right, and finally

4) Brian promised to clear Mila and LoCheVa of any wrongdoing and to clear his name and their name at the same time.

She drove to downtown Reno and arrived at her lawyer's office and walked in, and Ethen blurted out,

"We are in a deep load of trouble."

"I know!" Mila exclaimed.

"What happened?" Ethen asked.

"I don't know. I knew something like this would happen."

They both sat down for a moment and Ethen picked up the phone and called the DA's office and Paul Carol's deputy attorney clerk answered and Ethen told her the news. All they could say on the other end is that they would investigate the situation.

Ethen hung up dismayed.

"Where is that document Brian signed?"

"You have it! In your files"

THE APPELLANT

Ethen opened up the case files and found the document that Brian had signed and looked it over.

"This will have to do. I really wish we would have got his declaration through the lawyer you hired."

"I know. Yet Warren could not get Brian awake. He was heavily sedated with morphine from what he noticed."

Ethen realized there was probably a good reason why the medical facility kept him heavily sedated. Without Brian's testimony, they had no chance to defend and win, and the State would default to their investigators testimony and Mila's case had no star witness.

Mila and Ethen finished their meeting and discussed next steps and had to wait for the DA's office to get back with them.

Ironically, while Daniels was in the midst of helping Mila, he was also getting to like her. Something strange happened next; Daniels found out Mila had a boyfriend named Alex.

Oddly enough, Ethen immediately changed his stance and distanced himself from her and requested more money to defend her.

This was not what Mila expected, having her lawyer change his demeanor and his terms when her having a boyfriend had nothing to do with her case.

Undeniably, Ethen changed his tune and pulled back from the case and suggested she find another lawyer. Mila was not pleased but she could do nothing about it.

MILAGROS RAYRAY

Chapter 18 – Change in Legal Defense

Mila realized that now she had to start over and find another lawyer and she could not get back any of the money she had already invested, yet Ethen had her files made ready for her to get another lawyer and part ways amicably.

Changing gears once again, Mila received a referral from another caregiver and business owner who was charged with elderly abuse and neglect.

This caregivers' name was Hannah and she recommended Harold Lawson. Mr. Lawson had defended Hannah for a similar incident a few years back. According to Hannah he was one of the best of the best and effective lawyer when it comes to this kind of case.

It was a Monday morning and Mila along with Pia went and spoke with Harold face to face and explained all the details to him on what and how it was happened piece by piece moment by moment. Mila gave him the documents and files Ethen's law office.

Harold was very assured that this case was a piece of cake. Brian's fall was just an accident and Brian "was alive and well" when they transferred him to Reno Living Care.

Mila and Harold agreed how on the legal fees to go to trial and to defend Mila to the best of his ability. Mila provided Harold $15,000 to start the legal process and to start investigating all the facts as well as all the witnesses involved on this case. Mila gave Harold the letter that Brian wrote and signed that the fall was just an accident nothing more.

THE APPELLANT

Harold was very confident about Mila's case telling her that most of the cases he handled before were much more serious, brutal. Her case was so well documented and if it went to trial she would win. Her case was a simple slip and fall. To be charged with Abuse/Neglect and Exploitation was absurd. Even if Brian had made her the executor of his estate she should not be crucified like what she was experiencing.

Mila agreed with Harold's comment "what a drastic punishment". Mila kept asking and telling Harold to please subpoena all the families of her residents because they were the ones who knew everything about her care. Harold told Mila that she had nothing to worry about because this case was a slam dunk in comparison to all the cases he had handled before.

So Mila gave her his complete trust and just let him do his work because he gave her his re-assurance that this case was just a piece of cake. Ironically, she could not be further from the truth.

What happened next was unthinkable.

There would be a two (2) year delay from the time of indictment in September 2006 to the plea deal in October 2008 and then to top that off, just thirty days from declining the plea deal to a November 2008 trial. What just happened? What was the back story from two years of investigating, to a plea deal, and then a slam dunk and trial to a possible innocent or guilty verdict? Which way would it go? Mila's lawyer and the district attorney's office had to know something was going wrong. Was something in those plea negotiations that needed to be revealed to Mila?

It is tendered that the prosecution needed to build a case against Mila over those two years and somehow find a way to lose the star witness in her defense.

To get the ball rolling, the State immediately revoked her business licenses before the end of 2006 without proving guilt and forced her to remove all her patients and because of her inability to do business and earn an income, she had to let all her care givers go, and short sale and get rid of all her LoCheVa properties; three in all.

Across those two years, she was trying to pull together resources to mount a defense. She lost three of her houses and all her patients and clients. She was running out of money fast and could not sustain everything. Mila was stressed and very unhappy.

In the midst of Mila's legal defense, her legal counsel was planning on a plea deal as the outcome for which Mila had no intention of accepting. She believed in her innocence.

Before Mila's trial the District Attorney office headed by Attorney Paul Carl offered Mila and her defense attorney a plea deal and bargain. It was a plea bargain the DA believed she could not refuse: 6 months' probation if she pled guilty to all charges.

That was not going to be the decision Mila decided. She knew she was not guilty. There was no fault or guilt. However, Harold was in the midst of wanting to accept the plea bargain and the DA's deal when Mila informed him of her counter decision. Harold was not prepared for Mila's disagreement and rejection of the deal. He was actually very upset. He wanted all along to do a plea deal.

THE APPELLANT

Mila had already made up her mind, not guilty or no contest to anything. The DA immediately reiterated and warned her to accept the offer: (6) six-month probation only if she pled guilty. She re-iterated to her lawyer, "no and hell no".

This had all come about even after taking away Mila's license and her three residential care homes and moving all her residents to different home care. Mila had nothing left; her identity as well as her livelihood was taken away from her for no good reason. In spite of it all the DA had the nerve to offer her a plea bargain that he expected her not to refuse.

But she did refuse without knowing in advance her own lawyer could betray all his promises and his reassurances made to her. For him her case was just a piece of cake if she would accept the plea deal. To actually go to trial he probably did not bargain on. Mila's case was just an accident that led to a simple fall, and the industry knew that slip and falls happened all the time especially to the elderly either in the care of family or caretakers.

When Mila turned down the plea deal her lawyer Harold started telling her that she probably made the biggest mistake of her life and she asked him "how so?" Harold told her that no matter how good her case was he cannot guarantee that the outcome will be in her favor. Mila told him that all she needed from him was to do his job and to represent her and defend her to the best of his knowledge and his ability; that was all.

Mila even asked and begged Harold to subpoena all her clients involved especially Brian who was her only hope and a critical witness to this case. Harold told her that there was no need to do all that even though he knew these people were very critical witnesses to her case.

Mila even separately hired Attorney Warren Carlson just to get a legal statement and recorded voice statement from Brian. She even begged Harold to subpoena Attorney Carlson to be a witness on her behalf. Harold agreed to subpoena Warren, yet during the trial Warren was nowhere to be found. Something was going on behind Mila's back and she knew it.

Mila was frustrated. She asked her lawyer Harold "Who are you? What kind of lawyer are you"?

Harold had indicated that he had made an oath to defend her and the people, and to do his job to the best of his ability, knowledge and heart. She was amazed he was not committed to her cause as deeply as she had hoped. He had promised and made assurance to Mila for her not to worry that this was just a piece of cake.

What really happened to all his promises and money? When Mila went to trial she even begged Harold to put her on the stand because she did not have anything to hide. Mila wanted to tell the Judge and jury what really happened and how it happened. Mila was seeing and predicting this trial was going to be her worst nightmare and she was right and her lawyer Harold was not doing his job at all.

Mila needed a miracle. It was not going to happen, at least not now.

THE APPELLANT

Harold's negative thinking kicked in and he realized the State's one good way to get rid of a witness was to keep them heavily sedated until they have a heart attack or just give up and die. Whatever was to happen now, it was going to be an uphill battle to defend Mila and LoCheVa.

Mila's defense strategy was now going to have to take an abrupt change. Their star witness that Harold was going to be using is now dead, and the written statements could not be corroborated by a living person.

The State and County DA started their investigation without remorse and would probably end it that way completely up to and through the trial regardless of the truth.

To the reader, this is how it really works. One is guilty until proven innocent and the defendant's resources are locked up or depleted in comparison to the State's unlimited resources. Mila would not be able to defend herself properly.

For Mila, upon suspicion of any wrong doing from the State opinion not proven facts is willing to immediately freeze and remove a suspected wrong doer of their ability to defend themselves with adequate resources. For Mila, her livelihood was removed in order to mount a strong defense. Her business and medical licenses of all LoCheVa's facilities were revoked, and in doing so, all patients and residents had to be transferred. No patients, no money, no strong defense for her case. The State was quick to dismantle the years that Mila had worked to build a successful, trustworthy and honest business.

This was not going to be the end of the State's actions. They did not have enough to pin manslaughter on Mila but they had enough from secret testimony that was incorrect to now continue to file charges without the key witness alive to protest. The State was more than likely going to be successful in their mind and plans. What the State saw was one thing and it was completely wrong based on the facts and the testimony from all residents and patients of LoCheVa. In order for the State to succeed, it was going to have to apply pressure to all those on the defense in order to have them flip-flop their original investigation answers and lean against Mila. The State and County DA was readied and willing, and with unlimited resources and the power of the pen and their state seal behind them to protect them.

Mila's legal defense team was unprepared for the onslaught and her eye witness account and existing patient testimonies were the only defense she had to protect her from the State's investigations and nearly unlimited resources to mount their prosecution. With Brian's death the State and the County DA now did not have to worry about his testimony.

Brian's testimony could have caused a reversal of all their actions against LoCheVa. A reversal would have cost the State dearly in defense reimbursements, re-instatements of business licenses and payment of incurred income and losses, and quite possibly professional ethics violations committed by the State against LoCheva. Did the State overreach and grossly error and behave as in misconduct consistent with gross malfeasance of anyone in the public or private sector? Yes? No? Maybe? Probably? Most likely?

The bottom line, with Brian dead, LoCheVa was easy to dismantle and have Mila's life and livelihood torn apart. What was about to happen next was going to get even uglier for Mila's life.

THE APPELLANT

Chapter 19 – Wronged by the Jury

As the jury was summoned and convened Mila knew that her defense was weak. Her lawyer Harold Lawson wanted Mila to take the plea deal yet she knew she was innocent.

The day for the trial came and the defense and prosecution completed their statements and legal procedures.

Note to reader: this is where a great court battle took place and the defense did a pretty good job yet the defense witnesses were swayed by the prosecution to flip their story and go against Mila. It was evident that most of the defense's witnesses and testimony had been pressured to switch their stance in the wake of their professional careers and businesses being dragged into a defense that no matter what, they did not want to stand for or against.

The jury only took a few hours and the verdict came back. "Guilty!"

Mila was lost. Painfully lost and hurt!

She even knew juror twelve was biased when the verdict came back. Juror number (12) twelve was completely biased with seniors; she even testified and told the Judge as well as everybody present in the courtroom. All the Jurors including the Judge just ignored that comment and the statement from Juror number 12. Mila's lawyer challenged the court but the judge still refused to disqualify juror number 12 for any reason.

Judge Alan Bridges refused to agree with Mila's lawyer even when challenged. The judge's bias did not change the fact that this was a clear violation of her constitutional right. This wrong decision by the Judge and the jury impacted Mila's life drastically because the verdict was GUILTY. Her life had already been shattered and now it was being destroyed even further. Mila's entire life was changed by the people and the unjust system that was blind to the truth. How can someone go to jail and prison for just a fall who caused by an accident and the victim was alive and well and was killed in the Skilled Nursing Facility before my trial? How sad, and painful to know that a person like Mila who was never been in trouble with the law was going to spend (5) five years in prison. Mila could not comprehend what kind of a justice system in the world exists to have this happen to her. What kind of jury and district attorney's office would send someone to jail and prison for just a slip and fall, an accident and then after (2) two weeks in the hospital was discharged alive and well. Brian died in a skilled nursing facility under the control and observation of the State and he still died. Most likely it was due to constant morphine that elevated his risk of heart attack and that was the cause of his death; cardiac arrest – not a slip and fall.

Regardless, Mila had to pay for a crime she did not commit. She was likely to go to jail and prison for something she did not do. The prosecution, namely District Attorney Paul Carl was a wolf and predator when it came to justice or in the case of Mila, delivering injustice.

Mila would experience a very sad and very painful process of being pulled away from her children and leaving them behind, along with her grandchildren and her families and friends for a long time.

The worst part of Mila's nightmare had just begun.

THE APPELLANT

Chapter 20 – Sentenced and Unexpectedly Jailed

The day of sentencing arrived - 9AM January 21st, 2009. Mila arrived at the courthouse and her appeal lawyer Quincy Taylor was nowhere to be found. Her trial lawyer Harold Hoskins was there. The sentencing guidelines were simple. The judge only needed to have the prosecution and the defense present for the sentencing to take place.

Mila was under the impression her appeal was being processed as she approached the defense side of the court room. She was unaware of what was about to happen. Again, she thought and realized her appeals lawyer was not present. The courtroom was sparsely filled from previous and ongoing cases.

The prosecution came in a few minutes later and approached their side of the courtroom. The District Attorney Paul Carl was smug in his appearance and body language. He knew the sentencing and he knew what was going to happen. Mila and the defense would not be prepared.

"All rise" said the bailiff. Everyone in the courtroom stood. The judge walked in and seated himself.

"Be seated" said the judge said and everyone sat down. Across the courtroom he looked boldly and on this day Mila was about to learn that she was not going home as she expected. She was expecting to hear her sentence and go home and visit with her kids and prepare whatever was to come.

The judge looked through his papers and up across the courtroom. The court reporter was sitting and poised for the judge's next words. Both the defense and prosecution was seated quietly. Mila was nervous that her lawyer was not present.

The judge spoke, "Bailiff". The bailiff said, "All rise."

MILAGROS RAYRAY

The judge spoke again, "In the case State versus Milagros RayRay, you are found guilty of elderly abuse, neglect and exploitation. You are hereby sentenced from to 2 to 8 years in prison with the possibility of parole after 2 or 4 years. You are so ordered to start this sentence immediately. Are they are questions from the prosecution or defense?"

The prosecution replied, "No your honor."

Mila spoke up and replied, "Your honor, my case has been appealed and I did not know I was going to jail today. My appeal lawyer is not here yet and he told me he had filed the paperwork."

The judge replied, "Mrs. RayRay, your appeal is not before me and the court. Your lawyer being not present is not an issue. This is a sentencing hearing."

"What?" Mila replied. "That cannot be." Her face went cold and empty. Mila did not understand. The judge did not have the paperwork to keep her from going to jail immediately.

"Bailiff, please take the defendant into custody." The bailiff and two deputies approached Mila and she was stunned. She did not know what was happening. They officers asked her to stand and she almost refused and started to cry and speak out. She looked back across the court and her family was not there. They thought she was going to court and would be home afterwards. Mila was alone and now being hand cuffed.

The judge looked across the court and this being the last case of the day he said, "This court is adjourned" and slammed down his gavel. "Bam!" The sound of the gavel chilled the courtroom and the judge got up and left the courtroom as Mila was being asked to turn around and her purse her other lawyer was taking from her along with her jacket and folder. She was in shock and to make matters worse she was alone.

THE APPELLANT

Chapter 21 – The Parr County Jail

It was 3PM January 21st 2009 and Mila was at the rear of the courthouse after just being handcuffed and being escorted to a holding cell and she was crying and scared. She had no idea that she was going to jail this way. No chance to see her kids or do anything she had planned that afternoon at home. She even had a patient waiting in her car parked down on the street believing she would appear and be released to go through the appeal as her attorney had promised.

It was a nightmare. The sun was going down and she could barely handle her emotions. The sheriff deputies who had handcuffed Mila had put her in a holding cell inside the court house until the other remaining prisoners were also processed. Mila's clothes were getting messy and her wrists started to hurt from the coldness of the handcuffs.

"Milagros RayRay", a sheriff deputy belted out.

Mila looked up from the floor. She was desperately trying to figure out what to do. Her face was distraught and she did not know if anyone knew where she way. Her family and kids has just seen her earlier in the day, and now; she was locked up.

"RayRay! Let's go". The deputy barked out.

The deputy opened her holding cell and escorted her out and she was taken with others to a van waiting in the back of the court building, and loaded and driven to Parr, the County Detention Center. It was not far away, but a lifetime for Mila as she looked out the police van.

At Parr, that's what everyone called it, not just Parr Boulevard, Mila knew things were bad but it would only get worse. She was treated like an animal, like a murderer. All the jail officers appeared to have no sympathy and no care as she noticed their scowl, look, and forceful pushy behavior. To her they acted like god and they owned that world. The day ended with her losing all her belongings and clothes and placed alone in a separate cell. She made one call and that was allowed to let her family know where she was. The day ended for her in total emotional darkness.

    The next few days Mila were slow and scary. Time stood still and the jail was gloomy, dark and cold to her. She did not sleep. She only quietly cried.

    Mila spoke to her family almost every day until she realized her phone bill was over $500 for the first month. The jail did not tell her the cost of making phone calls was going to be so much. She hated it. She was miserable.

    Finally after a week, she was able to see her family and that was the worst moment in her life, her kids seeing her incarcerated and behind bars, and looking the worst she ever had in her life. She did not want to visit with her family again until she was free. That was going to be a long time to come.

    For nearly a month Mila just cried in her cell and did not eat. She did not know why this was happening. Her lawyer Quincy Taylor was quick to visit her. Mila's legal requests for bail pending appeal were denied. Her lawyer tried relentlessly to get her freed on bail pending the appeal but Mila was considered a flight risk. The judge just considered her untrustworthy. Why would she be considered a flight risk and untrustworthy?

    For no good reason she was denied. She was distraught. Quincy visited her three times while all attempts failed with the court. The district attorney's office and the judge would not grant her bail.

THE APPELLANT

That was it, pending all the costs of litigation and she was nearly out of money. She had borrowed money from her friends and family to get a good lawyer and to no avail. She was going to be transferred to prison and have to figure out how to continue her defense and gain freedom from there.

Mila's stay at Parr was over. She never wanted to go there again. Instead of being freed on bail for her appeal, she was scheduled for transfer to the state prison, scared and alone.

MILAGROS RAYRAY

Chapter 22 – The Transfer to Smiley

The day came – Mila's transfer to state prison. She was going to be transferred to the women's state prison in Las Vegas. It was 6am, the guards woke everyone up in the detention block and told them breakfast was ready. Mila got up and looked around. She had not slept that night either. She was in a cell by herself. She was only wearing a dark blue jump suit that was very uncomfortable. One of the guards came to her cell and unlocked it, told her to get up, and said she was to be transferred to the state prison in Las Vegas, aka soon to be learned as Smiley.

Mila just stared at the guard. Mila knew this was coming. She got up, and looked around. There was nothing really in her cell that was worth remembering and taking with her. It was just sad. She was empty. The three months at Parr was nothing in comparison with where she was headed. All her freedoms, thoughts, memories and valuables were fading fast and feeling gone. She had her kids in her mind and heart and she longed to be with them.

It was no use. Mila got up, walked out of the cell and down the corridor with the guard. She looked over and saw nine other inmates assembling in a line and it seemed everyone was headed the same place, the same prison.

She got in line and they handcuffed her and put on a thick leather belt around her waist and then shackled her ankles. The guards ordered them all to walk in a line and out to a yellow bus that was parked outside the building. All ten of them were being escorted slowly herded like cattle. In the detention area, the onlookers just stared and said nothing.

Mila got onto the bus, slowly stepping up without losing her balance and letting the chains and shackles get caught and snagged. It

THE APPELLANT

was not easy. Two guards on the bus, one man, and one woman yelled at them to get seated and the guards came by and locked them into their seats and told them it was going to be a long trip and not to get anxious. Mila looked out the window and noticed the clouds and mountains. It was going to be spring soon and all she could think about was losing her life and family, her pride and respect.

The bus pulled out of the Parr facility and started to make its way down US 395 and as they headed south crossing through Reno. Mila looked to the left over to Sparks where her homes and family were and just stared until she could not see the area anymore. She was starting to cry and her chest was hurting. She knew things were all wrong. She should not be here. If only Brian was able to testify and all the patients who should have been heard by the jury and judge – it was not so. A bump in the road made Mila snap out of her glazed over stare. It was partly cloudy as the bus left the Truckee Meadows and headed south, going through Carson City and onwards to what she would soon call her home for who knows how long; two or eight years: a lifetime in itself.

She looked down at her hands and noticed how dry they were and her nails were cracked. Looking at her reflection in the bus window only showed the image of a woman who looked exhausted, worried, tired, worn out and afraid. All Mila could hear in her head was the words and sounds of the judge, jury and prosecution who ruled so harshly against her. How could they for someone who had no previous criminal history and now going to prison. What a very harsh sentence.

The judges and jury should have ruled in her favor offering probation or innocence versus a guilty verdict; even a no contest plea. A guilty plea was not correct for she knew she was innocent and everything was made to look like she was guilty. She was not.

The bus kept rolling and Mila's thoughts were in turmoil. She knew arguably that the state had unlimited resources, time and power and she had all her resources especially money stripped from her by the State. There was no way she could defend herself. The investigations were twisted and the defense witnesses flip flopped their testimony based on intimidation from the State's investigators. The defense witnesses needed to preserve their own professional careers instead of testifying for Mila and the truth.

Mila's mind spun out of control just thinking about all the wrong done against her by the State and the District Attorney's office. Time was not important anymore.

Almost an hour passed while she did not even look around at the other nine prisoners. Nor did she look at the guards. The hum of the bus going down the freeway was of no comfort. Mila shook her head and closed her eyes.

It was almost 9am when she realized her stomach was empty and she was thirsty. There was no water and of course she had not eaten in days because of the stress. She looked forward and asked the guards if there was any water. The guard yelled back that they could have some in a few hours at the first stop; in Tonopah to pick up more headed to prison. Mila thought that would have to do. She had no choice.

When the bus finally arrived at Tonopah they pulled into a secured yard and were unchained from their seats and escorted inside the detention facility where they were unshackled and given a chance to relieve their bladder and were given some food and water. It wasn't much but it was better than nothing. Mila started to notice the other girls that were with her.

One was very young, maybe 18 and another looked very old, maybe in her 70s. Mila was just 50 and she had never seen a jail cell

THE APPELLANT

let alone prison. Mila was still processing all the unpleasant smells and changes in her last three months. As she sat there with the nine other prisoners, four more were joining them, all she could think of was being a business woman and helping so many to being suddenly chained and locked up seemingly forever; her kids was all she tried to focus on. Her middle daughter Cherise was about to graduate from college, and Valerie her youngest was just nine years old, and Lot, her oldest was just married. Mila was so ashamed and mad, troubled and pissed off, scared and weary, all those emotions at the same time.

The guards within 15 minutes said it was time to get going and got them all in a line and shackled them up again and had them get together in a line outside. Again they boarded the yellow bus and got seated and locked down. The bus lurched again and headed down the highway. They were only half way to the state prison just outside of Las Vegas. As Mila rode along she would occasionally look at the mountains and realize her freedom just kept slipping away. Mila was so tired and had not slept for a long time. The three months at Parr she only slept occasionally, maybe a few hours per day. The sounds at night in the cells listening to the others talking and whispering, the guard's footsteps, the cells opening and closing, locking and unlocking. Would life get any better at a state prison than a detention facility? Mila had no idea.

There was one more stop on the way and they would not allow anyone to get off. It was more or less for picking up packages and deliveries.

It was 5pm and the yellow bus arrived in the outskirts of Las Vegas and slowed down a bit while the traffic increased on the highway. The prison Mila was transferred was on the east side of Las Vegas and not far from the main freeway. It was hot and windy and the bus swayed a little in the blazing heat waves. All the prisoners onboard were not saying a word except one could see them all sweating. It was like arriving at a cemetery and everyone was going to be buried at the same grave site.

The main gates to the prison opened as the bus slowly came down the road named Smiley. Smiley Road would be the name that Mila would have in her mind for the rest of her life. She would learn no one refers to the prison other than to say they were at Smiley.

Inside the prison yard, the bus pulled up and a dozen guards were standing outside and waited for them to come to a stop. As the bus halted, the two guards inside got up and yelled for everyone to get ready. This was there stop and that everyone was getting off.

Mila's heart started to quicken and she was frozen in her seat. The guard came up to her and unlocked the chains from her chair that was keeping her in place and told her to get up. Mila did as she was commanded and stood there as the rest of the prisoners were unchained. They all slowly shuffled down the bus aisle to the door and got out and sun was blazing down on them and the heat was choking. They scurried over to the building while the waiting guards were yelling at them to get inside and to not stop. Mila had no intention of stopping because the heat from the concrete was scalding her feet.

Once inside the building everyone was brought into a line and a guard with a clipboard yelled out to respond if their name was called. Each name was yelled, and Mila's name came up and she yelled back and the guards looked up at her and stared. For just a moment their eye contact was frozen and then the guard kept going. Once the roll call was finished they were all unshackled and told to go into another room that looked like a giant locker room.

THE APPELLANT

Outside and inside there was a mixture of male and female guards, but in this room only big strong and muscular female guards were standing. One of them yelled out to get stripped and to throw all their clothes over in a basket for a physical examination and check for lice and any other things that would be detrimental to their inmate incarceration and in-processing. Mila was shocked to see the others girls slowly undressing and the guards just stood and stared. Mila had no power whatsoever to stop and decline. She did as she was told and undressed and was totally naked and standing there in the room like the others. Some girls had tattoos everywhere, piercings in weird places, and then a few looked rather normal like her but just as worried and new to prison.

The in-processing was embarrassing and degrading. Mila wanted to just hide and disappear. No one should be treated like this. A doctor came forward and said that she would be stepping through the line-up and inspecting each prisoner for their hair, ears, eyes and mouth, armpits, as well as the customary turn around bend over and spread your cheeks. After that, everyone would need to shower and get fresh prison clothes. The medical inspection only took a few minutes per prisoner and then everyone was told to go to the showers on the opposite wall in the locker room.

Mila took her shower and the water was cold, refreshing in comparison to the heat but still embarrassing taking a shower with some twenty other women of all ages.

When done, they were marched butt naked down a hall and stood in line to get clothes, a dark blue jump suit that would barely fit right, but it was a temporary clothing solution to get them covered up. What happened next to Mila was her prisoner number assignment. Her prisoner number was #128255. That would be her number for the next two to eight years. She had better get used to it.

MILAGROS RAYRAY

That number would be the only way the outside world would be able to reach her, by her booking number aka her prisoner number. Mila just could not believe how anybody could stand to be treated like this. She wanted the day to be over but it was not. She soon was taken to a room where the other prisoners were told to sit down. One by one, each of the prisoners were called by name and taken into a room and given packets unique to them and explained what was going to happen to each of them.

When everyone was individually counseled, the main group was given an orientation by the warden who came into the room and introduced herself. The warden basically said why they were here, how the prison system was supposed to help them with their rehabilitation and that if there was anything anyone needed to contact her through the guards. That ended the day and each of them was assigned a room and a cell within what was called a pod.

There were two beds per cell. The color of the rooms was crème color and in each pod were 40 inmates, so basically 20 rooms. The day ended at 11pm and not soon enough for Mila was exhausted from all the adjustments, cell changes and the above all else her clothes fitted terribly. No one knew where she was and her family just knew that their mother was somewhere far away from them and it was going to be a long time before they saw her again or hear from her.

All Mila could do was pray: pray hard. Pray softly. Getting in-processed at the state prison was absolutely embarrassing. Mila was full of bitterness, full of dreadful pain and kept asking God how did this happen and how did she get involved in such a drastic mess like this.

She realized again she had to be strong and fight the good fight of faith for the sake of her children, and her grandchildren and all her families. She kept telling herself not to give up, not now and never, as long as she knew the truth; the truth would eventually set her free.

Mila soon planned that every day she would keep praying, asking and begging God to please make her into everything He wanted her to be. Eventually Mila would soon fall deeply into His word and everything about Him. She wanted to feel His presence His majesty all around and through her. She wanted to hear His voice, and have Him talk to her and comfort her. She wanted Him to take away all the dreadful pain she was going through and eventually He would.

The transfer to the state prison was the beginning of a new journey of her life and the scars it would apply to her soul, her life and family would never be forgotten. The memories and time away from the ones she loved would be hopefully remedied in the future through God's will.

She could only keep her faith while at Smiley. Smiley would be her new prison and that would change shortly as well, after all the pain, the suffering – there would be acceptance of her fate but not the immediate forgiveness of her accusers and prosecutors. Behind closed doors, Mila knew the truth and God did too.

MILAGROS RAYRAY

Chapter 23 – The First Years – No Parole

The first year passed by slowly. At first one month passed then three, six, then one year came. Mila missed all her holidays, her family's birthdays, weddings, anniversaries and babies being born.

Mila had only one visitor at Smiley and that went uneventful. She did not want her family to see her there let alone visit her. She was so ashamed. Yet after a few months she became accustomed to the daily routine.

Eventually Mila's probation hearings came around. She was granted a meeting with the parole board, and she was asked simple questions like if she was accepting of her guilt and was her rehabilitation in prison working. What did she think about her prison sentence? Was she guilty? Was she not guilty? Her response was not guilty and she pleaded with them. The parole board continued her sentence as "Parole Denied." Mila was declined parole and she could not understand why she was in prison. For her, this was the first parole hearing and of course, she still believed that she was innocent, and committed no crime, no harm, to no one.

Mila kept asking herself "Why me". All the blessings she had been receiving were from God. She had always shared her blessings with others and to the less fortunate, and she always helped her patients. She knew that her conviction was not due to being guilty but due to the fact her defense was incomplete. It would be years later that she realized that the law was not perfect. Not all jurors, judges and legal professionals were equal and honest, and ethical.

"Why me?" she asked herself time and time again while in prison. She had always helped her patients, her families here in the

THE APPELLANT

US and her families in the Philippines, some of her nieces and nephews to shoulder all their finances all the way to college. She even bought a big house for them in Paranaque, by the International Airport. Was it wrong to work hard and serve the elderly so caringly and so faithfully that somehow the system would find fault in her ways and life as to strike her down.

For many days, weeks and months she walked quietly through her prison confinement with that thought, "Why me? What did I do that was so wrong? She knows she did nothing wrong.

Thinking through all the pain and misery, Mila wanted her family to taste and enjoy some of rewards from her hard work. That was coming to fruition when she was accused of crimes she did not commit.

She wanted to share all the blessings she was receiving from her Lord Jesus Christ. She wanted her family to know that she was forever grateful for taking care of her mother during the time of her absence and also for showing all the loves, the comfort and cares she deserved.

Mila knew in her heart that God had bigger and better plans for her life because "He is the only witness behind closed doors" He can make a way where there seems to be no way. She really believed with her whole heart that God's will - would be done. She believed that His word does not come back void and that He still is on the throne and He is sitting at the right hand of Heavenly Father. What happened to her and her family will impact the whole world because she would be a living testimony and would reveal His glory to the world in His time. It would be His will.

Chapter 24 – Reasoning through It All

What was Mila going to do about her life and her situation? Should she just surrender to man and the system? Let man and the system take everything and leave her nothing. Was God watching? Should she fight the good fight of faith knowing that God was with her and know that He will never leave her nor forsake her. She could be bitter and vengeful but no she would not in order to rise up for His glory, because she knew that in the end she will see the end of the tunnel of her current path and find the new path that God has promised.

This justice system would not allow her to make her case and plea yet at the same time nor would Mila allow them to dictate her future and final destination. In the midst of the prison sentence she knew she must find patience, wisdom, reasoning and the path towards happiness in His eyes and through His will.

This justice system she would reveal by her own hand in how they mishandled her case. Mila would reveal their injustice and failure to understand her defense and appeal, and to help reveal other victims who were scrutinized and poorly understood and represented and defended against false accusations. With all the help of her Holy Spirit she would do all things through Christ who's strengthened her.

Did Mila know at the time in prison that her future was being written by Him to reveal to her that the past would be forgiven and also healed by Him? Through Him she would take and turn those who had wronged her and give them a chance to make right what they did wrong to her and many others.

This was one of the reasons why Mila would write her story, and open up a series of books to reveal to the whole world how the

THE APPELLANT

justice, medical and legal system that exists can be improved rather than less exist and be than tolerant and understanding, fair, kind and understanding.

Mila wanted the whole world to know how her defense team could grow and improve, and the prosecution could improve rather than gang up on her and pin her down, strip her of resources and ability to defend. The system had worked so hard in order to convince the Judge and jury that she was guilty, when she was not.

Where was the justice? Was the world just about money, quid pro quo, tit for tat, concessions and trade-offs?

Should an innocent take a guilty plea while not guilty because the prosecution does not have enough to convict, but enough to make life painful, and the defense does not have enough resources to continue their defense, yet must concede the State has unlimited resources.

The reasoning through it all, from the outside looking in, from the front side looking at the back end, the fight for innocence while innocent is worthy even if found guilty through a flawed system. The State has chosen unwisely yet was correct in their ability to control the outcome and the final decision of the defendant even if only for a while.

Only behind closed doors does the truth exist. For Mila, she knew that her fight from the beginning was sincere. She knew her helpfulness was not to end in vain. Brian was the only one who knew the truth, and she did too. Other patients, neighbors and friends knew Mila for who and what she was.

While this break in the story exists, the reasoning from the beginning to the end shall continue to show you the truth of her innocence. She lost everything and retained that which was most important; her faith and belief in herself to help others.

MILAGROS RAYRAY

Mila looked out her cell window which wasn't much to look through and just stared blankly. Two seasons would pass before anything would happen that would help her cause.

THE APPELLANT

Chapter 25 – Behind Closed Doors with God

In October 2011 after serving nearly two and half years something extraordinary happened to Mila. She had an encounter and visitor from someone she had known as a child only in church, bible study and her prayers.

This was the first time in Mila's life that God actually came and visited her. He spoke to her so loud and so clear. God came to Mila's side and presence at 4:00 AM while she was lightly asleep on the bottom bunk in her cell.

Jesus appeared and moved to be within her room while she was facing the door asleep on her side. He knelt down by her side and whispered to her, "My child. Have you heard the good news?"

Mila opened her eyes wide in astonishment and gladness, and replied, "What is it my Lord?"

Jesus replied, "You are going home Tuesday."

Moments passed and Mila batted her eyes in disbelief and Jesus nodded and smiled at her. She was mesmerized and comforted in his smile and presence. Jesus stayed with her for a while and then slowly said he must go and he would be back soon, and would watch after her and send her help.

Mila drifted back to sleep. After that encounter Mila felt like she was on top of the world. It was a blessing, a privilege and opportunity to be a chosen one. He had continued to say to her that many were called but few were chosen. To be chosen from God to be one of His ambassadors was an amazing revelation.

WOW! At that moment Mila was very determined to fight her case all the way knowing that God was with her and she knew that in her heart that "HE can make a way where there seems to be no way."

The words GOOD NEWS to her symbolized that He put a promise in her life and that promise she knew in her heart would come to pass. Our Lord Jesus Christ promises not come back void. His will would come to pass. She just had to be patient.

That morning Mila went and called all her children and families telling them that she was going home on Tuesday, and of course they were very happy and excited saying finally after so many years of sacrifices, many years of dreadful tears pain and suffering, but again the question was "when". Mila told everyone about the encounter she had with Jesus Christ, and she explained it to them that it's going to be Tuesday and indeed she went home Tuesday like her God said. Yet it would be a little longer in the future than she had hoped for. A Tuesday in the future it would be.

In the meantime, Mila petitioned and appealed her case to every court and she would continue to send her plea to every federal, district, and the appeal court that would listen. She was relentless.

Jesus Christ was the only witness **behind closed doors**.

THE APPELLANT

Chapter 26 – The First Appeals, et al.

It was December 2011 and the years had passed by and Mila's work as a pod porter helped with passing her mind, keeping her in shape, and allowing her to consider and reconsider her time being served and parole hearings. Mila was happy to be at Smiley for a few reasons. For one, she had never had so much rest in her life. All her life was work, dedication to helping others and serving so many with needs. For her, though against her will, she only had to focus on her love for God, her family and children. She needed help and her money was empty and low, and her family was just able to help her with her books and basic amenities. At Smiley, many of her co-inmates loved her. Though she was locked away, she was still free and safe. She was ok.

Something was missing, something was not right. Each petition though accurate seemed not enough. What was missing? Mila asked herself why she can't win if God is on her side. Several public defenders took her case by request and order of the court by her petition.

Each appeal was responded with Denied! Denied! Denied! That is all she heard and read. The court's positions were upheld yet she was grateful her consideration was allowed. That is the great part of Mila's story was the ability to appeal.

Moments in Mila's life were passing and she had been waiting for a positive response; wanting, and wishing for what may come and when it did, the answer was DENIED.

Mila was very disappointed knowing she was not guilty, yet she did the very best she could and go above and beyond to take care of her patients and residents, especially Brian. At some point Mila did not know what to do. She cried out to God. She was very grateful and thankful to her Lord Jesus Christ because without Him she would not be able to live.

Mila prayed and begged for help. How would that come? She was not gifted to know some of the terms to be used in the legal justice system. Even her private lawyer in whom she completely trusted with her whole life deserted her. The last thing she wanted to do was mess things up more.

Therefore, she reached out and asked for her lawyer Quincy to help her finish her post-conviction appeal. That ended without success.

Mila's passionate pursuit to find truth was not without cost. She eventually could not afford her lawyers and in turn became indigent.

As an indigent, just the word sounded terrible, Mila could not afford to pay for the needed she needed the most. Her pride was gone. She just wanted justice and the truth to be revealed, and for the remainder of her appeals her status as indigent would help.

Therefore, she needed to be more legally savvy and know that to get things done; she needed to learn what most should learn, DYI Legally! Do it yourself (DIY) aka "pro se" and "in forma pauperis" would be something she needed to learn in prison and carry forward outside afterwards in order to carry on with her search for the truth and her eventual reversal of fate, and or pardon and restitution of her losses. This would not happen right away, but in the near present, possibly.

THE APPELLANT

Chapter 27 – The Appellant is Created & Born

It was a sunny Sunday morning and the prison yard was just getting busy. Mila was in bed praying asking God for direction. She needed help and so many months had passed and nothing was happening great in her life. Her prayers to God seem unanswered. Was she still all alone on the inside?

As she got up and started to brush her hair and wash her face, something miraculous came to her mind. She was nudged, and realized something or someone was going to get help and she did not know how. A messenger would come and help her she thought. For whatever reason she did not know but there was something coincidental about to happen.

Mila looked in the mirror at her face and deep into her eyes and something caused goosebumps on her arm. She shivered and was warmed all over. She was puzzled and for a good reason.

Her cell mate, Rita, was just getting up too and started uttering strange words and Mila turned and looked surprised. At first Mila thought this was another abnormal morning but something strange overnight had happened to her cell mate. Rita was in doing time for something she would not say, but Mila thought she should not to be worried.

Rita got up and started to get dressed and then started to look at Mila strange.

"What are you doing with my stuff?" Rita blurted.

Mila looked at her surprised. "What stuff?"

"You know what you did! You're crazy!" Rita looked angered and flashed a stupid look at Mila.

Mila was just puzzled and the next thing she knew Rita was up in her space and pushing and shoving and before she knew it Rita started yelling and a guard quickly came to their cell and yelled at them both.

Rita just looked back and yelled at the guard that Mila had taken some of her stuff and was messing with her things. Mila had done none of that and for all Mila knew Rita had gone stir crazy.

"Both of you stop right now!" The guard yelled. The guard ordered them both out of their room and separated them. Within a few minutes another guard had arrived and both guards quickly decided to keep Mila and Rita separated.

The first guard yelled at them, "That's it! Both of you get your stuff, one at a time and get out here."

Mila did not have much and quickly grabbed her belongings and piled it in her sheets and pillow and rushed outside the cell. Rita was dazed and looked crazy and did not want to leave the cell.

"Rita! Get your stuff and get out here now!" The second guard barked. The guards were not going to tolerate any kind of fighting or violence.

Both Mila and Rita were ordered to separate and relocate to different parts of the prison. Smiley was not that big, but big enough for the time being to separate two fighting prisoners.

The other prisoners just looked on and looked away like it was normal. Since the prison had about 20 complexes and each complex housed about 40 inmates, Mila could be transferred to any one of them. Mila landed within twenty minutes in another pod and was quickly taken into another group of women inmates that were absolutely strange to her and her to them. It did not matter, that was the norm.

During that transfer Mila crossed paths with a lady named Wendy Burke. Wendy was in for murder and she had some experience with the law and paperwork. What that meant Mila was

THE APPELLANT

not sure. It was not every day Mila runs into a person who had killed someone.

Note to the reader, this is where Mila is created to be the Appellant for the rest of her life. Take note, this does not happen every day. Mila's story was about to take a new turn. She was about to get a jolt into the legal process from the inside, but it was a side that she needed to learn but from an unexpected source.

Two weeks after being transferred from one pod to another, and as pod porter there, she met Wendy, and this is what happened.

Mila was slowly pushing a cart through the common area and this lady was sitting at a table with a stack of paperwork and some books.

"Hello, who are you?" Mila asked as she was starting to clean the pod area, pushing her utility cart through the area that had nothing but a mop, sponges and bucket of cleaning water.

Mila does not just randomly begin by running into the table of a lady sitting in the common area and just going through paperwork and a packet of seemed like notes, lots of notes.

"My name is Wendy" The lady replied, looking sharply at Mila and then back at her paperwork.

"Hi, my name is Mila. Nice to meet you"

Wendy was not happy about being interrupted, but she realized that a newbie in the pod was always a welcome sight.

"Mila, what are you in for?"

Mila was slow to respond. She was tired of cleaning and tired of long hours as a pod porter, but it helped with her books and her seniority, and kept her mind busy.

Mila replied, "Elderly abuse and neglect."

"That sucks." Wendy replied.

"I know." Mila said

They both looked at each other and Mila was not sure what to make of the meeting other than she was new and Wendy had been there a while and working ravishing on some sort of paperwork.

The day ended, and Mila and Wendy noticed each other on an off again. The next day would be no different.

Mila had just become adjusted to her new pod. Wendy was in another area and somehow they were meant to meet, per God for an unknown purpose to them at the moment.

The next day started and Mila got up and started her day, getting some breakfast, coffee and looking around at her new surroundings. Most of the new inmates she had met were aware of her books and liked the fact that Mila shared. Simple things like coffee and beverages, and other basic items was a nice thing to share with others Mila had thought. Mila was lucky. She had family and friends able to provide her with putting money on her books and that allowed her some of the nicer things to make her stay more comfortable.

She had been at Smiley for more than two years and she was realizing her fate knowing she had to do something. Wendy was constantly pouring through paperwork and books while Mila kept cleaning and doing the regular pod porter work.

Finally one day while running through her normal activities, Mila had to stop and ask Wendy what she was doing.

"Wendy, what are you doing?"

"Mila, I am trying to file and win an appeal on my case."

"What do you mean?" Mila asked.

"I mean, I can file paperwork without a lawyer or with a court appointed defense attorney for my appeal. It's my right."

Mila was puzzled at this information and revelation. She could do the paperwork herself and ask for assistance in doing so.

THE APPELLANT

It was a matter of moments after this realization that Mila knew her life was now in her hands. All this time she believed she needed a lawyer to do the paperwork. Mila would become her own author, writer, reviewer and editor of her appeals. She just needed a library with legal and lawyer stuff in it. She needed a pen and paper, some forms, stamps and envelopes. This is where she would begin.

The Appellant was now born and created; her name was Mila.

MILAGROS RAYRAY

Chapter 28 – Mila's Appeals, Denial after Denial

It was the end of 2012, the three years slowly passed and Mila made the best of her sentence. She had gone before the probation board twice and she knew she was innocent, yet they did not budge. They would see her good behavior yet they were nonetheless moved until she had completed nearly 50% of her 2 to 8 year sentence.

For the probation and parole board, they did not know the entire story before her indictment, let alone her pre-trial challenges, and the delays and denials, let alone the plea deal prior to the trial twist of fate, flip flop of defense witnesses and more. The entire process did not include the motivation of the secret witnesses to the prosecution and the district attorney's office internal challenges that only a few knew of during those years.

Mila completed all she could in 2012 for her legal appeals and it was not easy. Though she tried and tried, her filings would be in vain. Another whole year would pass and she would be just the same where she was at. All she could do was wait out her time and be on good behavior, be a pod porter, and stay true to herself.

2013, just another year and though she was not 4 years past, and the fourth year of being confined she knew the parole board might finally let her go and offer her parole. She was not sure, but she did have a lot of chances since her good behavior and excellent pod porter work. Many of the inmates loved Mila and the guards did too.

It took a year between appeals to different courts, filing this and that, and continually hoping that her requests would be heard.

THE APPELLANT

The process was not easy. The paperwork needed to be filed just to be able to file an appeal was laborious. All the Latin terms needed to be learned to represent oneself "pro se" along with court appointed counsel was not an easy task.

Mila's frame of reference was changing while she was preparing to be released. Instead of being a 3rd person to her story, she now was going to be released and become a 1st person to her story and lead the way forward; however possible her life after release and probation might unfold. She had her faith. That is all she needed.

PS. In the near future, all of Mila's appeals were supported and processed by many public defenders of many sorts. To her it came as a surprise that 4 years in the future a retired lawyer would come to her attention and willing aid her in her research. That public defender did not really remember Mila's case or appeal, but confirmed her ability to confirm that mass incarceration of those innocent or guilty are stripped of their resources to defend themselves appropriately. Mila's research would not go unnoticed and while everyone involved wished to remain unlisted and unnoticed in this story, the story must go on and the truth must be revealed.

MILAGROS RAYRAY

Chapter 29 – Released from Smiley

The day had finally come for me to be released. It was 8am May 27th 2014 and my night long sleep passed quickly. I looked around my cell and knew that for the last five years it was something I grew accustomed to and though I did not have feelings good or bad, I knew that my memory of this moment I did not want to remember, or did I? I was like a bird in a cage being finally set free. The others who were still going to be there would they miss me? Would I miss them? For each of them, I am sure seeing me get ready and leave was there wish as well.

My belongings were packed on my bed and my cell was neatly sorted such that my mattress and pillow and a blanket were all that was left. I walked down to get some coffee for the morning and others were looking at me knowing this was my last day. I said good morning to them, got my coffee and said a few things to my friends. A few gave me a hug and the others were just sad to see me go. We started out as strangers in cells, and then over time had become sisters in Christ.

It was about 9am when I left the breakfast area and back to my cell and looked around one more time. My emotions were so tender and sensitive that walking out I am not sure I would remember each face that looked at me while being out processed.

It was now 10am and I was called by the prison guards that it was my time to go. The walls around me and each hallway where the bars opened and closed as I was escorted to the yard and entrance seemed cold and gray. The colors of everything I looked at seemed to just blend together. I walked to the bus and got on and each inmate to be released joined me and sat down with their belongings. Our few belongings which what we had gained over the

THE APPELLANT

years was loaded under the bus. I looked out the window and towards the prison and saw others in the yard and I wondered how much longer each of them had to serve and be there. Some would be there for a few more days and others a year or a lifetime.

It was 10:15am, the bus started and we pulled out of the entrance and through the fenced gates and slowly turned down to the freeway. The sun was shining and a slight breeze was coming from the south. The trees looked wonderful as they lazily stirred in the summer heat. It was hot outside, about 95 degrees and while the bus was air conditioned I knew it was going to be hot when I got off. The ride to the bus station took about 15 minutes. Downtown Las Vegas was a bustle and I had not seen it for nearly 7 years. The cars were different too; newer and more flashy colors. The bus pulled into the Greyhound station and most of those released got off except for a few of us that were headed to the airport.

Mila's niece had purchased an airline ticket for her and Shannon, Pia's cousin, and her new baby girl was going to meet and pick up Mila at the McCarran International Airport that was only thirty minutes from the prison that Mila had stayed for five years. The airport was one of the busiest airports in the US and of course finding Mila where she was going to be dropped off might be a problem.

Shannon arrived at the airport terminal and made a few passes around the airport until she found the terminal and gate where Mila was going to be dropped off by the prison bus. The time for pickup was scheduled for 11am. It was 10:45 am and she was a little early. She pulled up and parked with her flashers on so that others would know she was going to be there for a few minutes.

The prison bus pulled up to the terminal gate ahead of where Shannon had parked and she noticed that the bus was nearly empty. She saw a few heads get up and start to move towards the front of the bus as the bus door opened and a prison driver got out and opened the side luggage storage on the side of the bus. Only a few pieces of luggage were there and one of she could see was probably Mila's. Mila was the second person off the bus. Shannon noticed how different Mila looked and though she knew her aunt was strong person, she could see that five years had taken its toll on her. The freedom of enjoying sunlight and fresh air was missing from her aunt's figure. Hopefully that would return quickly.

As they sat there in the car, both Shannon and her baby girl were waiting for Mila to see them. Shannon's baby girl was only 2 years old and would not remember this event, but Shannon knew she would. It had been a long time since Mila had seen Shannon.

Mila got her luggage and looked around and then saw Shannon open her car door and get out and wave and Mila smiled and picked up her bags and walked across the sidewalk to the curb where Shannon and her daughter was waiting.

"Mila!!!" Shannon yelled out.

"Shannon." Mila replied.

Mila just smiled at first outwardly and cried internally holding back her emotions. While Mila had spent the last five years of her life trying to appeal her case, she realized that being on the inside of Smiley was a vacation from the rat race and the real world.

Mila wanted to go home and get back to her children, and though they might be and could be ashamed of her, she loved them very much. Her pride and all she had worked for was gone, long gone.

Mila and Shannon got into the car and went and found a Filipino restaurant not too far away. Shannon had brought some of her own recipes and the restaurant owner knew of their planned

THE APPELLANT

arrival and made the exception and privacy to care for their own kind and nationality. Mila was actually thankful for the kindness yet it was not necessary. She just wanted to get on the plane and go home.

Shannon and Mila shared some moments for at least an hour prior to the time for her to head back to the airport. Mila had not seen the inside of a car for nearly 5 years and adjusting to riding and seeing the outside world was grand and hurting all the same.

Regardless, Mila needed to get going and Shannon had issues of her own and had been instructed by Pia to pick up Mila, share some moments and eat, and give her a plane ticket home from Las Vegas to Reno. Only a few hours passed and Mila and Shannon parted and Mila got on her flight and came back to Reno to rejoin her family and pick up the pieces of her life.

Chapter 30 – The Continuation of Faith

Back in Reno, every day of Mila's life she had put God first before anything and she surrendered everything to Him knowing He is the only one who can help her with her situation. Her flesh so many sometimes tried to convince her that it was time to give up. Was it time for her to realize that God was not listening to her anymore? Mila kept fighting every day to remind herself not give up. She had always remembered all the "Promises of God".

Mila's things were slowly brought back to her, and she did not have much left after all the years in prison. Most of her belongings from the three homes were lost, sold, given away.

She was still the Appellant. She was able to rent a house with her families help and start to figure out what she could do to continue her search for the truth in an appeal. The next few months and years were not going to be easy. All she had worked for was lost and forfeited.

She kept reminding herself just stay focused and look up and look at all the things that were created by God Almighty. If He could provide food for the birds, the lilies and all the animals then He would provide for her. Mila did not have much but He provided everything she needed…everything.

Sometimes when she prayed and just talked with Him she cried because she did not know how to thank Him. What an Honor, what a blessing and what an opportunity to be a chosen one.

THE APPELLANT

Chapter 31 – Probation Time

It was June 2014, and Mila was on probation. Mila's probation lasted less than six months and probably due to all her good behavior and work while at Smiley and maybe some folks on her side in the system that was well aware of the situation and the entire story.

Mila's probation officer (PO) was thankful for her continued efforts and while she tried to gainfully get work, she ended up having medical issues with her breathing. It was not nice and it was not easy. Regardless, she wanted to work and return to having a healthy life. For Mila her life would take a long time to return to happiness and find hope in her life. God only knew what could happen and if she had faith in him, that was all she needed.

It was now December 2014 and she did not even want to think about Christmas. She loved the Lord and honored the birth of Jesus yet she could not get a grip on missing so many holidays with her kids. Her probation was coming to an end and she was finally set free yet she still had to finish up her appeals that were pending.

Her appeals she thought would be the solution to all of what she could do. That would not be the case because the system as documented was stacked against her. All she could do was pray and hope for a miracle. It would not come.

Chapter 32 – Highest Denial - US Supreme Court

This denial after denial was just eating Mila alive. The Federal Courts at all levels were supposed to look at and review all the facts, and the United States Supreme Court had the power to overturn the convictions if they would just spend time to read and analyze all the facts as well as all the statements from all the families of Mila's residents.

For the Supreme Court to consider, it must be of great public and social interest. The USSC had no idea that her case would be paramount as ever as the elderly cases continue mount a point where oversight and transparency would be deemed necessary.

Mila's case was typical for lower courts to handle and sweep under the rug. The plea deal was their easy way out.

Yet, USSC like politicians, only take action when critical mass has been achieved in the public domain. When a senator's child dies then long overdue action is taken. When a policeman or fireman dies then a judge or city takes action. Then why not when a caregiver is wrongly accused, sentenced and prisoned, why not does a judge take action, either in favor or against?

Why did Mila get denied her due process rights? Why would the investigation and prosecution refuse to acknowledge that this was just an accident that led to a fall?

What evidence was there to really pin her down and accuse her for such a drastic punishment? Was there a conspiracy at play early on in her pre-trial delays?

THE APPELLANT

Did Mila really deserve to go to prison for over five years of her life? What if her defense lawyers were under the same punishment, would they treat the case the same?

Mila also appealed to the 9th Circuit of San Francisco and the same response; denied. Lower court decision upheld and judges from all the same band and same legal underhandedness agreed against her.

Why did this court not see and review all the facts that could lead to Mila's innocence? Is it just how the appeal game works?

The USSC clerks were kind to Mila's request and quite helpful to let her know by mail and by phone her denials. Though she was not happy with the outcome, at least she knew there was a real human being on the other side that received her written requests and knew of her plight. She was grateful to them.

Ironically, the clerks of almost every judicial system are the fair and balanced ones who often see the failure and successes when the system does right or wrong, and they in turn have the ability to sway and help all parties come to a reasonable and fair solution.

The highest reviews and appeals were Mila's last hope, so she thought. Mila's story could help her in her plight and her ability to fairly and honestly reflect on her actions. The positive outcome might come reasonably if the USSC knew the entire big picture of her cause and her honesty.

For Mila, she was affirmed as The Appellant.

MILAGROS RAYRAY

Chapter 33 – So as it was lived, it will be written

Mila continued to live and enjoy her journey while still pursuing her dreams despite all her trials and tribulations. She had to make the best of everything for the sake of her children, her grandchildren and all my families who believed in her. Was it pride? Was it embarrassment? She worked so hard to get where she was and to have it all taken away because of an unjust system.

Mila told herself she will let the whole world know what really happened and it could also happen to another someday unless she shared her story and how they could prevent the very same from happening to them. If only she knew how at the time. It was not until she found in her future that writing about her story would both save her and others.

It was June 2014 and Mila started reaching out and sharing to everyone what really happened however much it continued to hurt and how painful and dreadful her life true story would end. She wanted all to witness from her in order to learn from it. These words of her life before during and after would be for the world to learn, grow and continue to share.

Mila today continues to grow and try so very hard to excel with the help of her faith in Lord Jesus Christ.

Mila decided to continue to live the life that her God designed and created for her. His will be done.

Months had passed since Mila's release and her probation soon ended. She was still trying to put her life back together. She had lost everything since her time in prison. She was now looking to get her life back in order. She had the help of her family, her sisters and

THE APPELLANT

nieces who were able to gather up her previous belongings from storage, at least what was left. She did not have much left. Most of her belongings were lost, and some of her things her family was able to use and other things she just did not care about.

Mila's transition continued uneventful for the moment yet she needed more help on her side to continue her fight and her plea with the courts.

The ending had not been written yet and she needed to be heard. The story was not complete. The truth about how she was unjustly treated by the State and courts was not yet revealed.

MILAGROS RAYRAY

Chapter 34 – Mila meets someone unexpected

Mila was single and a mother of three wonderful girls. Pia, her niece, told Mila to start dating and get back involved with the world. Mila had been divorced for quite some time. Mila had on and off again did some dating since getting out of Smiley, but nothing really came of it. She got close once and that was good but it was not the love she was looking for in her life. Her daughters were all grown except Valerie who was now only 17 years old and almost ready to graduate high school.

So she continued to look and see who she might meet. Mila's success at dating was here and there. She had several suitors that she liked. One was in California and the other was up in Oregon and another here in Nevada. Most of them were business owners who really enjoyed Mila's personality and wanted to get to know her more. Nothing really stuck for her.

One day, she was checking her messages on a popular dating sight and received a message from a man named Andy. The message just said "Hello. How are you?" Mila looked at his profile and it was basic, nothing special. He was local to Reno and a business man. His picture was so-so. He was a business owner like the others and he was about 5'8 or less and his pictures showed him as being husky. Mila liked husky and she wanted a man 5'8 or shorter, nothing taller. She also wanted a God fearing man, and Andy's profile listed "Christian – Other".

Mila did not respond to so many messages but this one seemed safe. So she replied and said "Hello. How are you?" A day or so passed and she came back and looked at her messages and noticed a reply message. It was from Andy. His response was "I am good.

THE APPELLANT

How are you? Would you like to have lunch?" Mila was happy to see a nice message like that.

She looked down at her phone and looked at a few text messages from a few of her suitors and many of them were asking her when she was coming to see them. She had traveled to a few and had spent time to learn more about each and visit with one of her relatives or daughters who were conveniently near. Oddly, it had been a while since she was asked for lunch and of course Andy was local to Reno. Hmmm she thought, why not. So they texted back and forth a few times over the day. Mila replied and Andy replied back.

"Sure. Where would you like to meet?"

"What kind of food do you like?"

"Any kind"

"How about Thai, I know several good places."

"Sure. How about Thai place in midtown, and there is one downtown."

"I like the one right near where I live, the one on 2nd street near downtown."

"That sounds great. How about 11:30."

"Perfect."

Mila and Andy met for the first time, and had lunch. The meeting was interesting to say the least. The table they sat at, and the moment in time and is now frozen in each other's memories. One thing led to another, and a first lunch led to another at a downtown casino buffet, which led to a moment where Andy noticed Mila and Mila noticed Andy noticing Mila, and the rest is now a funny memory and one you would love to hear, if you get the chance.

Fast forward to now as you read, and in this moment, Mila and Andy met and this book was the result of their encounter and many trials and tribulations each endured getting to know each other.

It was not a perfect courtship, but in God's eyes, it was just like He predicted. Each had a very strong Taurus personality, spiritual warriors and entrepreneurial leaders, and definitely persevering survivors, both broken and both able to help and mend each other from the inside out. Andy believed in their meeting was like two ducks. Each just happy to be with the other, do this and that, going here and there, and just happy to be around the other.

From then until now to the end of this story and their story, now you know how they met. Let's see how the rest of the world understands this book and how the rest of the world will review Mila's experience as The Appellant.

THE APPELLANT

Chapter 35 – The truth will be revealed

Mila was set out to reveal the truth, the whole truth and nothing but the truth. Even before she met Andy, she believed the truth would set her free. She wished that Brian was still alive so he could tell the whole world what really had happened at her trial, but he died in the care of the State. Did they overdose him to cardiac arrest? Was that intentional? Did her legal defense lawyers not see through the dogma and politics and see that the State needed to win through distraction, diversion, delay, denial and falsehoods?

What would happen if something in her case from the hospital or the courts was found during the course of clearing out and archiving her lawyers files by staff or subcontractor, either by accident or by intent, and was it meant to be suppressed? Does the person who discovers these files keep an innocent person out of jail and convicted: could it be determined as to be intentional or by accident. Was it overlooked, buried, and needs to be revealed so the system can correct a past mistake?

What if someone on Brian's side turns up something lost in their files that came through the mail that needs to be revealed?

What if one of the lawyers staff members uncovers something in their files that was thought to have been presented for Mila's defense and did not make it to the courts?

All of these thoughts and questions both pre-trial, while innocent until proven guilty, and then post-trial and post-conviction should have been taken into consideration yet the system is so focused on numbers and being right than just and truthful.

MILAGROS RAYRAY

Mila's class B felony was holding her back from so many things that she needed to do like get an apartment, find a home, get a job, and vote. All of those rights and abilities would most likely be held against her for at least 10 to 15 years. That could not be for Mila.

She was 59 years old and wanted to live a long and happy life but not in the US if the appeal, pardon and review board were sticklers for protecting their own decisions and justifications without a complete understanding of the truth.

Because of her faith and her fiancé, Mila's only hope was to request a pardon from the State Pardon Board or the US President. Ironically, she contacted each. For the next six months, and only the NV Pardon Board would listen and there were rules and exceptions that were requested, and though nothing other than their understanding, Mila hoped they would eventually understand her plight.

THE APPELLANT

Chapter 36 – The re-encounter with the defense

As the book was being written, Mila realized that she might need to contact her old defense attorneys in order to review, investigate, and gather their work notes and files for her case. Her fiancé was well aware of the need to review the files and make sure all the records and the book were succinct. The book was being based on a true story, her true story but if the facts could not be complete without all the details the lawyers might have.

The process to collect documents and all the materials her lawyers might have had was requested, yet ironically, the retention period for those documents, 3 years, had just passed when requested. How convenient.

Should the story become based on a true story, sort of? Would the real names and places have to be changed and become fictitious to a point to protect everyone involved? The latter became the default of the story, not necessarily the real names, but maybe streets and cities, and a few places that are of great public interest.

Mila did not want to blind side her defense attorneys and she wanted their blessings and support, and not any resistance or denial of writing and sharing her story. Therefore, her fiancé did some research on how to obtain the records based on the several attorneys she had hired and he developed a formal letter that would suffice to request the records.

Over a series of months, written letters, phone calls, and face to face interaction was completed with some success and some non-responsiveness. As those months passed between August 2016 to March 2017, and the legal defense lawyers were contacted including the prosecution DA. The results were mixed. The benefit presented to each was obvious, and the public could benefit from the process experienced. One lawyer was reluctant to respond until approached in person and presented correspondence. One lawyer was lost and absent without leave and suspended by the Nevada bar. Even the Bar had no idea where this lawyer was. Another lawyer when approached in all methods was non responsive. This lawyer was very crucial in their testimony for the defense and was conveniently absent during the trial as well. Another lawyer was so helpful yet said because of the Nevada bar code of ethics, they could not participate.

Oddly enough, the prosecution was still working in a public office and was polite enough to respond and call and discuss the possibilities and situation and was curious as to this book's final contents. So was the second defense attorney's final comment when confronted. It was good research to go back to the defense as best Mila's research could conduct, though she believed this research was not necessary, yet her counsel believed the ethics and taking the high road in the book and telling her story required due diligence and fairness. For Mila, she might not have been given the same fair treatment during her pre-trial, trial, and appeals, yet the planning, drafting and proofing this book required professionalism and leadership like all legal teams should be required to perform.

Did the requirement to approach the other witnesses about their testimony flip flop before the trial be needed? Absolutely! Yet the defense might have deemed that not necessary. While the medical teams and State's investigation teams were partly to blame, they were protected and more than likely to not comment unless anonymously, and only after this story was published and revealed.

Why did her legal defense team not subpoena the families of her patients for her character defense? Was this intentional again by

THE APPELLANT

the defense lawyers? Was this another issue with lawyers and their ability to ignore their client's wishes, requests and desires?

In the end, the greatest story and outcome is that the truth will be revealed and that of great public interest this story is shared so that another and others are better supported and defended.

What Mila learned in the process at the final end, is that the failure by legal counsel on either side is imputed to the client. Even if the client asks their attorney to do things the way they believe better, their attorney has no basis to listen or follow. In fact, the lawyers have every right to do things their way tactically and strategically regardless of how the client wants them to proceed. Is that correct? Does that make sense? Possibly somewhere in the Nevada Bar association and or Nevada Revised Statutes there is a clause to that effect. For Mila, the entire situation to this year of 2016 was frustrating yet she was making peace with it as the pages of this book began to take shape and her accurate recollection unfolded into type.

Her story while acute and painful was being balanced with prudence and caution because regardless of her feelings, thoughts and opinions, there were others who had theirs as well. While she could not absolutely be certain of the motivations of others, she was pretty assured that her approach and strategy while at the time was direct and hard, she was right. She needed a legal eagle yet how could she with little money left?

Even through Mila's the research in 2017 and her understanding of the district attorney's resume of previous elderly abuse cases handled, though only one reported, her case was his number two experience. That is not a good track record for him. Her defense attorney's record from her understanding was the same. Plea deal was the goal for all but not for Mila. She believed in her version of the facts and her understanding of Brian.

Out of the wood work came other complainants that took her one strike being held against her and expanded that if possible. That was not fair and not reasonable. The defense and prosecution should have found that to be true. She believed that everyone just wanted to distance themselves professionally from her defense in terms of their own defense for their livelihood and profession. Doctors and lawyers along with banks and their staff who were once on Mila's side and Brian's side quickly defected. Once the State applied their investigative pressure and seal of authority at them and their testimony and how Mila's actions seems suspect while not, their flip flop in defense testimony changed. How sad and unfortunate.

Mila wanted to be put on the stand to tell her story and be cross examined. Her lawyer refused. Mila wanted paperwork in her defense submitted to the court prior to trial, and her defense said it was not necessary. The case was supposed to be slam dunk easy.

The letter from Brian, the victim was not admissible because it was not hand written completely by him. It was a statement Mila had written up by Brian's own words and he signed, and the judge denied it as admissible. How wrong is that? Where's the precedent?

At the State, no one is rarely found guilty of failure to do their job properly because in the end, regardless of ethical codes of conduct and the revised statutes of professional rules, is a criminal case ever won? The State's goals are to win against the defendant if an indictment is pending. If the defendant like Mila had a lot of money and the State had behaved in gross error in their actions, then maybe Mila could have won.

The State and other divisions and departments of the prosecution had unlimited resources. While they might think not so, the State had the authority to hold, cancel, restrict, force and close actions and activities to anyone and any entity with or without being

THE APPELLANT

proven guilty or innocent. In the State's time and motivation would Mila's case and outcome be determined based on the political landscape and professional needs of those involved, not the truth.

Is the moral center of everyone in a legal profession a focus of their own personal gain and professional benefit regardless of the truth? One believes for the most part there are ethical people in the legal profession, but the system is designed to protect the professionals within the system, regardless of the situation. A defendant's plea and the truth at hand does not bend or curb the pain and penalty of the State's resources being applied to one harshly and unjustly even in the midst of false accusations, and an appeal process that is not client focused but process focused such that judges and their legal systems stifle aid, assistance and rectification.

The failure of the defense to reason with the prosecution without paperwork in play has always been today's dilemma. In the old days, tell it to the judge, and in these days, that is not the case.

That has been the dilemma between a legal defense and prosecution to know what is true or false based on facts versus investigative bias that lead to possibilities rather than what really happened and how events happened. While Mila was innocent, everything around her pointed to guilt through perception, or LoCheVa's staff's failures for which in turn she was ultimately responsible. This could have been the real reason for her prosecution and eventual prison sentence.

On the other hand, gross malfeasance within any organization and system as an outsider one cannot typically fight against. Typically what has been experienced and observed, the law protects the law. The law though made by mankind was designed with failure in mind, ergo the appeal process.

If man created, man can reverse create. Mila's defense had all the ingredients yet were not all used and prepared and executed in an order that could have saved her. The fact that the indictment as applied and the delays experienced in Mila's foresight knew the risks and stakes concluded drastic measures should have been applied, not the goal of a plea deal. This is where the failure of her defense lies. She could have taken the stand. The original letter of innocence and no fault from Brian who ironically perished in the hands of another should have been admitted as evidence clearing LoCheVa and Mila. The investigation evidence of defense witnesses should not have been caused and pressured to flip flop by the State's investigation team.

The lessons learned here are that Mila's story must be shared so that others may look hard at the case, the situation, both sides, through and through, ponder the situation of each individual, motivation of each individual, and put together the pieces and seek the truth. Find the truth and to do so, ask the hard question. Ask a hard question and expect a hard answer.

Judges are to seek the truth, protect the truth, and when the truth is evident should not dismiss the truth if not presented in the manner that law stipulates. Accept the truth and the evidence as received and augment the receipt of the information so that the truth is revealed and found. Counsel on either side should remain unbiased and follow the letter of the law, yet must really understand and apply the spirit of the law.

The law is alive and ever changing. The law has the history of case precedents and the changing times causes the law to be improved, reduced, and should be simplified. Of course some will always choose to complicate the law who wish to bend the truth for their own ends and motivation which is sad.

THE APPELLANT

Moving back into the situation of Mila's story, and in the case of Brian's last wishes – Mila knew he wanted to be buried next to his wife and not cremated. Did that occur? Was he properly buried or was he cremated? Who knows the real answer?

MILAGROS RAYRAY

Chapter 37 – Brian's Wishes

Brian wished was to be buried next to his wife Eleanor. Was Brian buried or cremated? Was he cremated and then buried next to his wife? One cannot be sure as of writing, yet Mila was 110% sure he was not buried as is but cremated.

Mila's pardon had been approved and her fiancé and her planned to visit Brian's grave a few months after her rights were restored. Though she had the majority of her rights restored, she chose to skip the 2nd amendment right to bear arms because it might have been easier for the Nevada Pardon & Parole review board to consider her point of view and truth rather than a full pardon. That would have been their decision and opinion. Sometimes rather than asking for everything, just ask for what one really needs.

The media frenzy had settled down after the story had broken about the real truth about Mila. Though Mila had contacted 20/20, 48 Hours, and Dateline, along with Oprah and Ellen, most of them were yet to reply. They were probably waiting for the book to be published. A few executive producers had contacted her and she had appointments to get back within them in a few weeks. She was not done yet with her final moments with Brian.

Finally the time had come to visit Brian's grave. It was a sunny Sunday morning in May, almost ten years after Brian's death when Andy & Mila planned to visit his grave. They wanted to place some flowers and close the chapter on the journey everyone had endured. Mila wanted to share with Brian that it was not his fault. Mila knew Brian wanted to come and testify on her behalf but cannot because he had been drugged to death by the system.

THE APPELLANT

Mila approached Brian's grave with Andy. She came to stand in front of it with her hubby's hands in hers. She looked up and over to Andy and said, "Andy, this is Brian. The man I tried to help and who set me free." She looked at the headstone and said to Brian, "Brian, this is Andy, my husband. I finally found the man of my dreams. May you rest in peace Brian - I love you."

Quietly and serenely somewhere in heaven Brian looked down upon Mila and Andy, smiling and knowing that her suffering would not be in vain. For without this experience, Mila would not have meet the love of her life, and his belief in her, and Andy's gifts of discernment, healing and foresight, and in doing so, finding the truth even if it was painful for even Mila to admit to him.

The day ended happily. Mila and Andy, Brian and their faith and love for the truth and of course balance of love and helping those all around us prevailed. Brian's wishes were met to the best of Mila's love and knowledge of caring and knowing him. All the other transgressions against her by others because of her desire to help Brian were pointless, mute and past.

PS. For you the reader, this is the end of Mila's story for now. For you and others interested in the intrigue, twist of fate, plot, and details of the story, please read on.

While this story is not complete and many more details and facts could be shared, this first release and version as a pilot for more to come is in our hands and your hands. If you know of others with a similar story and the need to share, contact the publisher or Mila directly.

MILAGROS RAYRAY

Chapter 38 – Epilogue & Moral of the Story

In the end the Mila served five years in prison. The two to three years leading up to her trial was completely damaging to her life and career. The years prior to her LoCheVa business and downfall were fraught with challenges, and struggle, yet she always focused on her kids and marriage as best she could. It was not perfect but it was all she had at the time.

Mila's final hope was in God and God alone. The predicament I was in was not a joke anymore. My case was denied all the way to the United States Supreme Court of America. I was praying and hoping I would get a chance for my case to be at least read and reviewed. After all the facts I had submitted there was clearly a violation of my constitutional rights. All the facts showed that the court didn't have any substantial evidence and the record shows that it was just an accident that led to a fall. Petitioner also alleges that the State Court conviction and/or sentence are unconstitutional in violation of petitioners 5th, 6th, 8th and 14 Amendments right to due process based on the facts/grounds found in exhibit No.1 and provided in Exhibit No 2.

Writing this story was giving Mila a huge relief to unload this baggage that she had inside of her, although she still vividly recalled the most painful and dreadful tragedy of what went on the whole time but she would not let this tragedy, these trials and tribulation dictate what she could and could not do. As long as she had God in her "greater is He that is in me than He is in the world"

Now Mila and her loving hubbie had decided to really concentrate writing this book and praying asking God to please send us and reveal to us the #1 author and publisher, and #1 producer to pick up this true story and send this message to the whole world and let them know what kind of a justice system we have and how really impacted someone's life because of this so called "Injustice System".

Her pretrial legal defense was the best money could buy and that is the entire basis of the verdict. She did not have enough money to mount a strong defense. The truth, facts and timeline of motive and reasoning behind Mila's actions was never presented in full and completeness to the jury on either side as much as she wished. The prosecution investigation revealed a completely biased position and not completely true.

Were there some wrongful actions and communications from the State's elderly services and investigation with the district attorney's office? Was there iffy handling between the investigators and the prosecution which created purposeful delays?

Was there bias from Brian's neighbors and family? Was there flip flop testimony from defense witnesses? Did a healthy elderly man die in the care of the State and that failure of care by the State get planted onto Mila? What if Brian testified? Would the State even allow it? Probably not; his testimony would unwind and disprove the State's investigation and goals.

Were the three different defense attorneys' not understand the gravity of Mila's situation until they realized they were incapable of defending her because she desired an innocence verdict, not a plea deal? By then after all the money was spread out, it was too late for the attorney's to return her money so that she could find legal counsel that would defend her innocence, rather than look for a plea deal.

MILAGROS RAYRAY

From the initial investigation to the indictment, and to the trial -- was that a setup against LoCheVa and Mila? Was the system and those involved sort of out of control in their role and experience in their profession for the times?

In this day and age, mass incarceration is a problem and the elderly abuse charges can be suspect at best in some cases, not warranted and biased from beginning to end.

Why are the local jail and detention center worse than prison? Mila's handlers and treatment at the detention center, if that is really a fair description, at Parr was by far worse than prison. At Parr, treatment was brutal and disrespectful and less than humane. Yet, at prison, treatment was fair and balanced, and on occasion a prison guard would get out of line but they were promptly corrected and removed from service by their own supervisors. Prisoners were already sentenced and their freedoms removed. Prison is a time for correction and reflection and not a time for more punishment.

In prison, freedoms were already removed. If you want to have someone return to society improved then the method of cruel punishment is not the way at the very first step of incarceration.

Detention centers like Parr could benefit from such advice and guidance on how to better treat detainees. Yet, on the other hand, maybe Parr has it right. How odd. The harsher the treatment to a prisoner and the sooner applied prevents recidivism and better yet a return to prison.

Whoa, where did recidivism come into this story? It has to do with repeat offenders and their likelihood to repeat their offense or any offense. For Mila, she did not know this term at first until Andy mentioned it with his experience with his work and all levels of

THE APPELLANT

law enforcement. Andy knew Mila would not go back and do that which she was falsely accused but the legal and medical field would not understand nor respect that. Her record had been tarnished and a Class B felony was on her record. That would hinder and halt her successful return to normal life without an appeal, pardon, or some degree of juris prudence and administrative motion and file of lost, misplaced, hidden evidence that was willfully or not and held up against and not provided to the jury and the courts.

Make this first incarceration experience as the worst ever such that prison is never a next consideration. A slight infraction and short term lightly sentenced citizen would never want to experience the Parr experience again. Regardless, Parr is not the place to be for anyone.

What if Mila had taken the stand like she told her defense lawyer she wanted to do. He refused to allow her. How odd, Mila believed she had the right to do so, yet her lawyer refuted her request. Ironically, the Nevada Bar and the State stipulates that the defendant cannot tell the lawyer tactics and strategy.

Mila realized too late that her lawyer was shooting for a plea deal rather than a real defense in her trial, and that would doom her. She did not have enough money to pay her lawyer to defend her after the plea deal was rejected. Did he not know she was against a plea deal? Mila ended up being stuck and that was really sad. That was the truth.

Her trial defense attorney Harold did a pretty good job yet in the end he lost and that was unfortunate. If Mila's witnesses and letters of support and her taking the stand had occurred, she might have had a real chance at winning. Even better, the letters and testimonies from her patients and residences family members should have been included in the trial for the jury to review.

Moving forward, Mila is a mother, an immigrant Filipina and a faithful believer in Jesus, God and her Holy Spirit that dwells with in her. She would not give up on her passions, and her heart's desire to help the elderly as she has always believed and done her entire life.

Her story and her life is not wasted on this story and telling it. Her pastors, her hubbie, and her family believe in her and love her. Was it painful for many of them to work through these last 10 years, the answer is yes. Yet, while one can admit there was wrong handling on all sides, Mila remains fervent that her story and her actions were right.

To this day, Mila is The Appellant.

END OF EPILOGUE

THE APPELLANT

Chapter 39 – Law Students, Judges, Investigators

This story is of great interest to the public and the case is rather easy to follow given the available facts. One could elaborate and expand as much as possible given time yet for the most part, this section is dedicated to the hope that law students, judges, colleges and universities consider the case for study and exploration regardless of their predisposition and understanding of the outcome.

Moving forward, open yourself to the consideration that this case was the first and pilot of an ever growing epidemic of mass failure by the system to properly handle medical and legal investigations of elderly care and abuse, and exploitation. Where does that leave you as a student? Are there cases that have higher precedent because of your law professors?

How would a law student understand this story and case if properly put into context, dissected, researched, eye witnesses interviewed, court documents scoured through, and the entire case history re-investigated? How would a television investigation team, daytime or nighttime investigation series approach this story and reveal the subtle and lost truth?

How could this book help the media for which our team approached on dozens of levels on dozens of angles both direct and indirect such that this story and problem for the public at large and looming did not interest them? That is puzzling.

For a law student, this book is fiction based on a true story. Only the key person is named Mila along with the location and the state in which this occurred. All other aspects of the case have been to the utmost extent fictitiously replaced other than the order of events and the timeline as best reconstructed.

If a mock trial with a mock defense and prosecution was to re-enact the entire story, how would that occur? Could that be achieved? Could it be evenly described in terms of what we know in case law regarding precedent and statute?

The table of contents for this book was created to aid with any reconstruction of the story in order to re-enact any or all parts of the challenges Mila faced. A law student can look at the body of work more easily, quickly and thoroughly as such. Is attribution required? Not really. Colloquial writing is allowed to some extent if the author is the subject matter expert, yet attribution can always be added.

For the legal and medical community, one is encouraged to look at the story and case of Mila both for and against and consider your stance and opinions. The truth will set her free as well as help you and others understand that all systems have flaws and all people have emotions and error.

The growing problem in the law and medical community is transparency into error and the cover up that might ensue to jail and imprison an innocent, as in the case of Mila's Story.

THE APPELLANT

Chapter 40 – Open Questions - Closed Answers

This chapter is dedicated in part to the investigation of Mila's case. Each and every case has open and closed questions that might help or hinder a case. For Mila, and her research team, what could help with the future of others in her similar situation? These questions though unanswered as of this writing, can help one gain insight into the legal and medical systems that exist. Improvement can be achieved, and successes of existing processes be continued.

The following questions are not in any order or precedent:

1. Are lawyers required to have ongoing ethics training throughout their career?
2. Why can't a group of lawyers as required by State law do pro-bono work hours per year as a group or team together to defend a supreme case appeal for an appellant like Mila?
3. Does the State Bar monitor and report to the public pro bono hours worked and completed per year?
4. How can the law, courts and law enforcement treat a defendant as guilty until proven innocent through an indictment? Is that fair?
5. Do prisons include a law library or at least free internet access to online law portals? If so, great. If not, why? There are not that many prisons. Why not justify at a reasonable cost the law library such that each and every inmate has the right to research their own case completely.
6. Why are visitation video conferences between prisoners and family members so costly? The vendor chosen, why? Isn't Skype even monitored and recorded nearly free?

7. Why are items through the prison system more expensive than the modern military PX? Shouldn't the price of coffee on the inside be the same on the outside?
8. Who gave the prison system the right for every vendor system to hike the rates on every product and service? Is that profiteering, price gouging, or racketeering?
9. Does the Bureau of Prisons follow the same federal guidelines for vendors as the rest of the federal agencies?
10. Does the voting record of the State Attorney General presiding at each and every Pardon and Parole Board hearing, always vote "No" or the "Negative" to each case heard even if the Governor votes "Yes" for the mere fact that if the AG did vote in approval it would undermine the AG's position as the police and law enforcement leader and those they lead?
11. Under the Constitution, is the defendant allowed to face their accuser? The State in this case was acting on behalf of Brian through their flawed investigation. Brian who conveniently died or was killed in the care of the State would have cleared Mila. A written and sworn statement to Mila's innocence Brian was legally and faithfully signed and then not permitted as evidence by the judge of the court. What a shame and total absence of justice and fairness in the beginning. Will karma prevail over the court's bad actions and decision?

From A to Z, are there more questions? Absolutely!

Should the law student and to be judges consider and debate possible improvements and move to have them made to exist in their lifetime? The brave answer is yes. The weak answer is no.

THE APPELLANT

Mila would love to have each and every person who reads her case consider her simple innocence and though the State can induce fear and induce psychological alterations against one's will through political and peer pressure, the fact that each and every one of us is human – the State tends to persuade in their favor.

Each and every one who held Mila and LoCheVa liable is forgiven yet not forgotten.

Only behind closed doors does anyone know the real truth.

MILAGROS RAYRAY

Chapter 41 – Timeline of Events – Important Dates

May 2006	Mila & Pia meet Brian & Harry for Evaluation
	Brian relocates to LoCheVa and loves it
	Brian's unexpected medical emergencies
	Brian's pre-existing conditions revealed
	Mila's considered giving Brian to another caregiver
June 2006	Brian and Mila work through his medical issues
	Medical staff supports Brian's stay at LoCheVa
July 2006	Mila and Brian and other patients continue to bond
Aug 2006	Brian's Slip & Fall at night, next morning to hospital
	Medical center staff investigates & misdiagnoses
	State gets involved and investigates wrongly
	Brian moved against his will away from LoCheVa
Sep 2006	Mila & LoCheVa are indicted
Oct 2006	Mila's & LoCheVa legal defense begins
	Mila is stripped of license
	LoCheVa unable to mount defense due to lack of $
	State stipulates guilty until proven innocent.
	All Mila's patients are forced to leave & relocate
Nov 2006	Brian's Dies –Cardiac Arrest at Skilled Nursing Care
…..	Two Year Lapse from Indictment to Plea Deal
	State builds case, delay, deny
	Defense believes slam dunk as innocent
	Medical & legal witnesses flip flop their testimony
Oct 2008	Mila & Legal Team receives Plea Deal from DA
	Mila Declines 6 month probation if pleading guilty
	Mila declines offer against lawyers wishes
Nov 2008	Mila's Trial – wronged by the jury
Dec 2008	Mila's Appeal – oddly incomplete
Jan 2009	Mila Sentenced – Thrown in Jail
Mar 2009	2nd Indictment Sentenced, Sent to Smiley 2-8 yrs.
2010/2012	Probation Hearings – Denied
	All forms of Appeals submitted & denied
May 27, 2014	Mila released from prison
Dec 2014	Mila off probation
Aug 2016	Contemplate book Mila's story, 1yr research
	Amicus Brief why not considered – too late
	Final USSC appeal denied; Mila crushed
	NV Pardon; Mila pardon exception requested
	NV Pardon Board attended w/Mila book idea
Nov 2017	The Appellant – released, counsel approved

THE APPELLANT

Chapter 42 – The Pilot Episode - Screen Play

The Plot

A Filipina immigrant makes the long journey to the United States, builds a successful business. Mila's care of a patient named Brian turns ugly when the greed and jealousy of Brian's estranged friends and associates turn against him and her. Brian, a lone surviving elderly patient nearing the end of his life wants to give his last will to his caregiver, and then accidentally slips and falls. The State harshly and wrongly accuses the Brian's care giver Mila of elderly abuse and exploitation.

The Conspiracy

The medical and legal system through systemic failures and overreaching and overreacting protocols wrongfully accuse and prosecute an innocent care giver. Medical professionals, lawyers, and witnesses are tampered with and coerced to change their testimony.

The district attorney's office was found to have an axe to grind against the defense attorneys and the Filipina culture for their invasion of the elderly and healthcare industry in the State.

The Twist

The State's investigation fallacies are revealed. Their agenda was revealed no increase in the State's 2003 budget and funding based on hearsay and innuendo, and false accusations to support their cause. Several in the State and County DA's office are found wrongful and guilty of gross malfeasance and abuse of power. Corruption is found between the State and County of an evil modus operandi.

MILAGROS RAYRAY

Chapter 42 – The End

Yes, we created a chapter for this so it could be easily found...

THE APPELLANT

ISBN BARCODE VOLUME 1 SERIES 1 ISSUE 1

ISBN: 1545370575
ISBN-13: 978-1545370575

Send Suggestions to:
Milagros RayRay c/o Mountain Publishing
490 E 8th St, Suite 200-C, Reno Nevada USA 89512
Calling Internationally +1 011 775-525-2830

Email to: MyStory@TheAppellant.com

MADE AND PRINTED IN THE USA

Final Draft by November 15, 2017
First Scrubbing by January 15, 2018
Final Scrubbing by February 15, 2018
First Feedback Improvements by March 15, 2018
Second Feedback Improvements May 15, 2018
Third Feedback Improvements June 15, 2018

To the researcher, within this book there are three Easter eggs. See if you can find them. Let us know.

The End

Although, for which I believe, there is no end. ...Amen...

www.ingramcontent.com/pod-product-compliance
Lightning Source LLC
Chambersburg PA
CBHW071423180526
45170CB00001B/205